Journalism

Polity's *Why It Matters* series

In these short and lively books, world-leading thinkers make the case for the importance of their subjects and aim to inspire a new generation of students.

Helen Beebee & Michael Rush, *Philosophy*
Nick Couldry, *Media*
Robert Eaglestone, *Literature*
Andrew Gamble, *Politics*
Lynn Hunt, *History*
Tim Ingold, *Anthropology*
Neville Morley, *Classics*
Alexander B. Murphy, *Geography*
Geoffrey K. Pullum, *Linguistics*
Michael Schudson, *Journalism*
Graham Ward, *Theology and Religion*

Michael Schudson

Journalism

Why It Matters

polity

First published in 2020 by Polity Press

Polity Press
65 Bridge Street
Cambridge CB2 1UR, UK

Polity Press
101 Station Landing
Suite 300
Medford, MA 02155, USA

ISBN-13: 978-1-5095-3854-6
ISBN-13: 978-1-5095-3855-3 (pb)

A catalogue record for this book is available from the British Library.

Library of Congress Cataloging-in-Publication Data
Names: Schudson, Michael, author.
Title: Journalism / Michael Schudson.
Description: Cambridge, UK ; Medford, MA : Polity, 2020. | Series: Why it matters series | Summary: "Why, in the age of Trump and fake news, journalism matters more than ever"-- Provided by publisher.
Identifiers: LCCN 2019042874 (print) | LCCN 2019042875 (ebook) | ISBN 9781509538546 (hardback) | ISBN 9781509538553 (paperback) | ISBN 9781509538560 (epub)
Subjects: LCSH: Journalism--Philosophy.
Classification: LCC PN4731 .S2485 2020 (print) | LCC PN4731 (ebook) | DDC 070.401--dc23
LC record available at https://lccn.loc.gov/2019042874
LC ebook record available at https://lccn.loc.gov/2019042875

Typeset in 11 on 15 Sabon by Servis Filmsetting Ltd, Stockport, Cheshire
Printed and bound in Great Britain by TJ International Limited

For further information on Polity, visit our website: politybooks.com

For Noah

Contents

Acknowledgments   viii

1 Introduction   1
2 What Kind of Journalism Matters Most?   13
3 Reported, Compelling, and Assertive   36
4 The Problem of Media Bias   50
5 Evidence That Journalism Matters (or
   Doesn't)   59
6 Why Technology is Not the Whole Story   76
7 Journalism's Four Non-Revolutions   90
8 Is There a Future for Journalism?   104

Notes   117
Further Reading   129

Acknowledgments

I am grateful to John Thompson of Polity Press for inviting me to do this book. Since the 1970s I have been studying and writing about aspects of the news media, especially the history and sociology of American journalism. Putting what I know or what I think I know about journalism into a form suitable for young men and women seeking a quick tour of the field, and in a way that might also interest journalists and scholars, was a challenge I was interested to take on. It would force me to articulate in a more complete way than I had yet done what I think about journalism and why I think journalism, at its best, is so important. I am grateful also to John for honestly telling me a couple of drafts ago when he thought I did not have journalism's story quite right.

Other trusted critics of earlier drafts include Julia

Acknowledgments

Sonnevend, my wife and a media scholar in her own right. Julia was the first brave soul to make her way through the manuscript. I am grateful to her for pretty much everything in my life but, in this case, for her intellectual acuity and honesty.

Polity's three anonymous reviewers were excellent – appreciative of the draft they saw but critical, too. Justin Dyer, Polity's outstanding copy-editor, cleaned up so many sentences I had judged perfect and clarified so many passages I knew were crystalline – well, dear reader, thank heaven you do not have to read what he did! Adelina Yankova, a current Columbia Ph.D. student, helped with some eleventh-hour research and offered astute comments on the whole manuscript. My former doctoral student and now director of the Reuters Institute for the Study of Journalism, Rasmus Kleis Nielsen, read the manuscript and steered me clear of some pitfalls. I have benefited again from his informed and realistic assessment of journalism, as of democracy itself, and about what these two institutions can – and cannot – achieve. My Columbia Journalism School colleagues and students are visible in the text and the endnotes and I am grateful to Nicholas Lemann for having persuaded me to join the Columbia faculty in the midst of journalism's digital transformations and the School's attendant

Acknowledgments

curricular changes. The very corridors of Pulitzer Hall reverberate with the ideals of journalism that this book tries to honor.

1

Introduction

It is hard to imagine a human community anywhere in the world, and at any point in human history, where people did not bring news to one another. Hard to imagine a setting in which people did not anticipate – with hope or foreboding or simple curiosity – news from travelers or others who had been away from the village during the day, or news from others close by with gossip to share.

But all human communities through most of the history of the species have managed without a specialized occupation for gathering and disseminating information and commentary on contemporary affairs directed to general audiences: that is, they have been communities without journalism. Indeed, historians typically trace back the origins of journalism only about 400 years, while journalism as a full-time occupation for a contingent of news-gatherers goes back only about 200 years.

For most of the human past, people raised families, worked the soil, gathered nuts and seeds and berries, established governments, conducted diplomacy, raised armies, went to war, developed religious beliefs and practices, built bridges and canals and cathedrals without headlines or tweets, reporters or editors. People wrote songs and poems, love letters and contracts, long before they wrote news stories.

Journalism has not mattered eternally but journalism matters. Many things matter enormously that are as new as or even newer than journalism. Consider electricity. Yes, people can live without it, as they did until about 100 years ago, and as many people in poorer communities still do. In the electrified world, some people intentionally live without electricity on camping trips or religious retreats. Still, most people most of the time in electricity-dependent societies would feel bereft without it. Power outages make normal life impossible even for brief periods. When there is an extended power failure from massive weather events like hurricanes or floods, or through extreme political dysfunction, it is an emergency. It puts lives in danger. There may be disruption of communications, destruction of ongoing experiments in scientific labs or of patient treatment in hospitals, looting in commercial areas, and accidents, crimes, and deaths in darkened homes and streets.

In the modern, urban world, electricity has become a necessity. But what use is journalism? Who really needs it? This is not immediately obvious, at least it is not obvious what journalism uniquely brings. Certainly it brings entertainment, but so do many other things, from video games to a deck of cards to watching or participating in sports to playing with our kids. It brings information, but so do teachers and coaches and physical therapists and books and many other sources. What does journalism do more than or better than or more uniquely than all these others in the information or entertainment it provides?

Some industries or occupational pursuits are self-evidently vital to a good society. Good societies need good doctors, teachers, bus drivers, supermarket cashiers, computer tech support staff, accountants, people with the skills to repair tractors or to prune trees. We depend on many people doing many different jobs every day, from the people who maintain a purified water system to the government officials who inspect the hygiene in restaurants or the safety of bridges and tunnels. The one part of journalism people regularly consult to organize their lives is the weather report. Weather forecasting in most places is undertaken by government agencies, but it gets relayed to the public by news organizations. It is a small element of what professionally gathered and distributed news workers pass on to the public, but people depend on it.

As for the rest of what journalism offers – who needs it?

And, with today's economically imperiled news organizations, who needs it enough or wants it enough to be willing to pay for it? If people are not willing to pay for it, could it disappear? And if it could disappear, why should any young person looking at the array of vocations in the world be foolish enough to pursue it? Is choosing a career in journalism today likely to be as ill-fated as deciding to manufacture carriages for the horse-and-buggy business a century ago?

These questions are not easy to answer. And journalists have not effectively explained the value of their work to the general public. Scholars who study journalism have not provided much help, either. They have generally been focused on or obsessed by the endless search for evidence, ideally quantified, of how a particular story (say, the *Washington Post*'s coverage of Watergate) or a particular journalistic cast of mind they disapprove of (for example, news that covers an election by focusing on the "horse race" among candidates rather than on the policy differences among them) influences public opinion and thereby the course of history.

If you can convincingly identify some bit of certainty or high probability that exposure to news media has altered people's minds and actions, that may be a noteworthy achievement. But I do not think these findings, here and there, from this study and from that, will ever tell us what we would really like to know about the power of the media because (see Chapter 5) they omit the most important, although most subtle, ways the news media make a difference in helping people come to a cognitive reckoning with a complex and changing world.

The world will survive without a lot of the journalism we have today, but the absence of some kinds of journalism would be devastating to the prospects for building a good society, notably a good democratic political system, or so I contend here. I want to champion in particular the production of original reporting that in both general and specific ways holds governments accountable when it is undertaken by reporters and, equally, photographers, documentary film-makers, bloggers, makers of podcasts, and others who operate according to the norms and practices of professional journalism.

Introduction

I will discuss what these norms and practices are and why we should care about them. In the past half-century, professional journalism, organized to tell true stories of contemporary affairs to, for, and sometimes with general audiences, has been particularly concerned to tell these true stories in a way that holds power accountable. In fact, this kind of journalism is now sometimes referred to as "accountability journalism." It is an apt term. I will give special attention to what this means.

I am not a journalist myself, but in my professional life as a sociologist and historian I have spent more of my time studying journalism than any other part of society. I remain an outsider, but I am persuaded by the authentic self-understanding of professional journalists (and, yes, it is a self-promoting position too) that journalism is not just a job but a vocation – that it has a public mission, with accuracy of reporting a chief measure of competence, truthfulness an overriding ethic, and a faithful portrait of the contemporary world as its objective. News should be compellingly presented to reach a broad audience even if it offers technical details that will mean more to insiders than outsiders. And unlike most journalism of the past up until the late 1960s, it should be, whenever possible, assertive journalism – assertive in investigating, assertive in analyzing, assertive in challenging people in seats of power.

All of this is easier said than done. Journalism in much of the world is in a long-simmering crisis – its central institutions are floundering economically, its popular appeal is under challenge from both new and old rivals, its self-confidence stumbles. The independence of journalism from state power is under attack in the global wave of populism where "strongmen," as they are known, vie for power or attain it and then seek to weaken or destroy any media outlets that dare criticize them. Under these circumstances, we need well-reported, compelling, and assertive journalism more than ever. This is the journalism that matters most – reported, compelling, and assertive, and I will elaborate on this model (Chapters 2 and 3).

A journalist's job is to make news, as a carpenter's job is to build houses. Both crafts have rules. The primary rule for journalists: put reality first. Responsible journalists learn to not produce fake news, hyped news, or corrupt news. They do not subordinate reality to ideological consistency or political advocacy. They do not curry favor with advertisers or with the publisher's business interests, or even with the tastes of the audience. Nor should they bow to their own colleagues if the consensus in the newsroom clashes with what they see in the world around them. This – the bias of the inner circle – is especially difficult to resist. What remains true about ethical journalism is just what reporter (and novelist) John Hersey said about it in 1980: "There is one sacred rule of journalism: the writer must not invent. The legend on the license must read: NONE OF THIS WAS MADE UP."[1]

"None of this was made up" means that all of it is accurate and that, if called upon, the reporter can defend everything he or she has written as true, as accurate. This is the most boring thing we can say about a news story – "it is accurate." But this is also quite possibly the most important thing that can be said. When Robert Pear, *New York Times* Washington, DC-based health care reporter, died in 2019, the *Times* printed a letter to the editor from Thomas S. Crane, a health care lawyer in Massachusetts, who remembered Pear's "complete dedication to detail and fairness and his breadth of knowledge of the politics of the health care industry." On one occasion when Pear asked him for some help on a story, Crane recalled, "We went round and round about a single sentence because of his compulsiveness for accuracy. After the third phone call that day, I finally persuaded him that the sentence was legally accurate and otherwise unassailable."[2] For a reporter, "a compulsiveness for accuracy" is very high praise.

A second rule for journalists is a good deal more complicated than it sounds: follow the story. Follow the story, don't follow a wish, don't hew to a line, don't submit to a fashion, don't go along with the crowd. Follow the story. To follow the story means that one cannot and should not anticipate where the story is going to go; one risks losing fidelity to reality if political, partisan, ideological preconceptions or loyalties block off the trail that may lead to "inconvenient truths," facts and patterns of facts that show one's favorite persons, parties, and causes in an unfavorable light.

Moreover, although Rule One – do the reporting, don't make stuff up – and Rule Two – follow the story – are both primary directives for professional journalism, they are in tension with each other. Don't make things up but do assemble the facts into a story that is not only coherent but also emotionally compelling. And that makes for a perennial battle between tedious, "eat your spinach" journalism and the stories that grab an audience and don't let go.

For a century now, a powerful trend in the world of newspapers, carried over also into news magazines, radio, television, and online news, has been professionalization. Newspapers emerged and continued for generations before any of them hired reporters, but from roughly the 1820s on in the United States, and a bit later in Western Europe, reporting became the central task of journalism. A French journalist, after visiting America in 1886, held that "reporting is in the process of killing journalism" – that is, in US newspapers straightforward accounts of events of the day – particularly events of the past 24 hours – dominated while in France discursive essays of political advocacy, theory, and philosophy held sway.[3]

But doesn't a passion for factual reporting fly in the face of the truth that presumed "facts" are just opinions in masquerade? That everything is relative, it just depends on the standpoint you start from? Most college sophomores walk into Philosophy 1 believing that "it's all relative." That's what makes them "sophomoric." And none of them actually believes that everything is relative. If their computer malfunctions, they do not pray that it be fixed by divine intervention, nor do they normally kick the computer (unless empirical experience has taught them that that works well). What do they do? They seek expert assistance. They may look for it themselves online or they may contact tech support. They actually believe there is an answer and it's not all relative. Some approaches will solve the problem and others will not. The computer works or it doesn't. The milk smells spoiled or it smells fresh or sometimes you are not quite sure and you taste it for a second source of empirical evidence, adding taste to smell. You certainly do not conclude that it doesn't matter because everything is relative and everything is positional and everything is subjective anyway so go ahead and serve the milk to your kids. We move through our lives figuring out what is real versus what is imagined, what is external reality versus what is a wish or a fear – every hour, every day.

What I will try to do in the pages to follow is to make a case for the utility of a professional journalism that seeks truth and chips away at it with a competent command of journalistic fact-gathering practices, turning documented facts into stories and analysis that engage an audience, and with an effort to assert itself rather than to defer to power.

In a reflective and illuminating recollection of his 20 years as editor in chief of the UK's the *Guardian*, Alan Rusbridger writes a dramatic chapter on the efforts of a Parliamentary committee to pinion him, if not imprison him, for his newspaper's publishing Edward Snowden's revelations of America's and Britain's surveillance of their own citizens. And he concludes the chapter with a sentence that begins, "You need proper journalism because ..." He leaves the sentence unfinished. He follows it with this: "But how did that sentence end? Because ... we are independent of other forms of power? Because what we do is in the public interest? If we couldn't agree on what the public interest looked like, how could we expect others to rally to that bedraggled cause?"[4] Rusbridger's unfinished sentence swings in the wind. This book is my effort to complete it.

2

What Kind of Journalism Matters Most?

There are many kinds of journalism. This has long been true, even though the digital environment is spawning a variety of new forms. Some pseudo-journalisms do more harm than good. Intentionally false, lying, malicious words or pictures about contemporary public affairs that pretend to be news about the actually existing world harm individuals and society as a whole. I leave these sorry fake journalisms aside. But there are various sorts of journalism that do good even if they are not the kind of broad public good made possible by the professional accountability reporting that is journalism's greatest gift and my primary subject in this book. Three varieties deserve brief mention.

First, a variety of forms of community journalism have the chief end of building solidarity in a small town, church congregation, a college, hospital, political association, or any other group that uses reports of recent news from and about the membership to demonstrate pride in that membership and the virtues of the community it represents. These newspapers, newsletters, alumni bulletins, and such link individuals to the greater whole in useful ways. Long-time executive editor of the *Guardian* Alan Rusbridger remembers starting out on the *Cambridge Evening News* in 1976, where the news editor reminded the novice reporters that every name of a local citizen inserted into a story sold a newspaper. "We were duly encouraged to cram as many names as possible into our reports. Every picture sold a paper, too, so photographers knew to take group pictures and collect the names for the captions."[1] The *Cambridge Evening News* was a more substantial news operation than the *Whitefish Bay Herald*, a weekly newspaper that, in the early 1950s, ran a photo of a group of pre-schoolers, myself among them, at a birthday party at Mrs. Gray's Nursery School. My parents clipped that photo and saved it for decades. It was, after all, published in *the newspaper*. "The newspaper" then gave anyone mentioned in it a stamp of legitimacy, as it still does in many communities today

This kind of community news typically offers a rosy or inflated portrait of the organization or community it portrays. Rather like a funeral eulogy, it offers a warm-hearted celebration rather than a report, even if what it says is truthfully told. I remember a very sensible, wry letter to the alumni magazine of my undergraduate college from an alumna who was reasonably content to read about the great achievements of other alumni trumpeted in each issue of the magazine, but, she wondered, what about most of our fellow graduates who achieve perfectly ordinary things in their later lives? Why not, she asked, offer more ink to mediocre alumni like me?

A second important kind of journalism is advocacy journalism. It does not tell us what has just happened or what is happening but what some writer or collection of partisans would like to see happen and what they passionately believe would be the best thing to happen for the world or for a particular community. This is a very common form of journalism and often a very useful one, not because it offers an original report of facts the public did not know but because it offers an interpretation of current affairs from an engaged stance that readers may find reinforcing or persuasive or perhaps challenging to their opinions about the world. It is one thing to report that the sky is falling; it is another thing entirely to propose how best to find shelter from that calamity. If primary reportorial journalism offers a portrait of recent events, advocacy journalism offers or implies a program of action. Many news operations incorporate advocacy as well as reporting, usually, but not always, separating the two so the audience can easily distinguish them.

In a third type of journalism, informational content is subordinated to entertainment. It brings news of interest to many without much of a claim to be more than diversion. No "speaking truth to power" here! Much of the news coverage that takes up sports, fashion, restaurants, and celebrities is entertainment journalism. This can be useful to individuals and it can also serve underlying social functions. Many people are deeply devoted to local sports teams and even to their news coverage. Few of these fans would contend that the future of democratic society rested on the successes or failures of any of their teams. Still, a shared sports enthusiasm may enable members of a community who are strangers to one another to chat civilly and enjoyably on the subway or in the check-out line at the supermarket.

We call all of these journalisms "journalism." All of them serve a variety of legitimate purposes. However, the kind of journalism democracy cannot do without, the journalism with the greatest potential for preventing harm to human liberties, justice, and the rule of law, is professional "accountability" journalism. This is the journalism that matters most.

Take a deep breath to prepare for just a few pages of history to help see how accountability journalism emerged.

In the nineteenth century, the British newspaper – like others elsewhere – was a miscellany, an assemblage of texts, each in a different voice. It was a depository for documents, often printed in full. It was a way-station for pieces reprinted from other newspapers, which themselves may have been reprinted from still others. Newspapers existed in 1800, but they rarely employed reporters. Even news stories about regularly covered sites like the courts or the legislature were likely to have been produced by a corps of writers located at the site they wrote about. These writers often sold their reports to multiple newspapers, but they did not have a desk in a newsroom of any newspaper. The pattern in Britain was matched by newspapers in Sweden, Germany, and Estonia.[2] The mid-nineteenth-century newspaper, as historian Donald Matheson observes of the British newspaper, simply did not "have a voice" of its own. It was a home for a variety of voices, few of them orchestrated by a reporter or an editor.

What Kind of Journalism Matters Most?

In a sense, journalism arrived at its own voice when it discovered quotation marks for the voices of others, setting them off within a single-journalist-voiced piece. It was at this point – in the late nineteenth century – that reporters did interviews for the first time and incorporated other people's voices into a "story" that the reporter controlled and narrated. It was at about the same time that news stories shifted from a strictly chronological account of some event to a story that began with a "lead" or "lede" that identified for readers what the writer judged most important about the speech that had been given, the vote that had been taken, the fire that had consumed a building, or the crime that had been committed. With the interview and with the lead, journalism acquired the literary tools, and implicitly the literary license that came with them, for what would be, in the early twentieth century, the professionalization of journalism.[3]

The world's first journalistic interviewing was undertaken by American reporters. Interviewing became common practice in the US in the 1880s and 1890s when the very idea of it still horrified visiting European journalists and intellectuals who observed these strange New World practices. Interviewing was strange in its presumptuousness – who was a mere reporter to ask questions of a

Cabinet officer? It was strange in its fact-gathering rather than literary or essayistic core. And it is no wonder that American reporters were the first reporters anywhere to interview the Pope, kings of European countries, and Cabinet ministers in Britain. The practice became far more general in the European press when American reporters in large numbers invaded Europe during World War I and showed their European counterparts just what interviews could accomplish.[4]

The formal professionalization of journalism in the United States can be traced to the early schools of journalism. "I believe in the profession of journalism," wrote Walter Williams, the founding figure at the first US journalism school, the University of Missouri (1908).[5] The second school, the Columbia Journalism School, opened its doors in 1912. Its founding donor, the prominent Hungarian immigrant editor and publisher Joseph Pulitzer, wrote eloquently about establishing a "profession" of journalism. He had the loftiest goals in mind:

> Our Republic and its press will rise or fall together. An able, disinterested, public-spirited press, with trained intelligence to know the right and the courage to do it, can preserve that public virtue without which popular government is a sham and a mockery. A cynical, mercenary, demagogic press

will produce in time a people as base as itself. The power to mould the future of the Republic will be in the hands of the journalists of future generations.[6]

Writing in 1904, about the time he decided to endow a school to offer instruction in journalism, Pulitzer declared, "I wish to begin a movement that will raise journalism to the rank of a learned profession growing in the respect of the community as other professions far less important to the public interest have grown."[7] But would this not establish journalists as a kind of elite class? That is just what he hoped for: "We need a class feeling among journalists – one based not upon money, but upon morals, education and character."[8]

This is the kind of journalism that Frank Sesno, former Washington bureau chief of CNN and now the director of George Washington University's School of Media and Public Affairs, had in mind when he suggested that there is a core to the field: "The DNA of news is to find a coherent story with a single, clear headline." That is far less lofty than what Pulitzer imagined. For Pulitzer, journalism was not yet but could be and should be a professional pursuit dedicated to the public good. For Sesno, speaking more as a veteran in the trenches than a commanding general, it is the craft of finding "a coherent story with a single, clear headline."

I like the "DNA" metaphor, but "a coherent story with a single, clear headline" does not exactly sing. It is no anthem to inspire new generations of journalists. Sesno himself acknowledged that his formula is not enough when the world is as complex as it is. When the news events before reporters are complex and a consensus on the right storyline does not emerge, then "the media will have to fight their own DNA."[9]

To fight their own DNA: why? Because the story will not cohere. The "single, clear headline" cannot be coaxed out of the available evidence. And still the reporter is obliged to tell a story, to simplify, to dramatize – to be perhaps a bit theatrical. The job of the news professional calls on the journalist to do all of this. It requires not only writerly gifts but also a feel for the audience and some analytical skills. The journalist has no state-certified license to practice nor a lab coat and stethoscope to establish authority. His or her exceedingly difficult task is to keep to the facts and keep to the story and at the same time set it in a context that gives weight to the underlying issues at stake.

Sesno's view of journalism is familiar to most journalists around the world, but nonetheless he describes as much a distinctively American take on the field as a generic and universal professionalism. Between the world wars, European journalists adopted some elements of American-style journalism, but Europe – especially France and Southern Europe generally – came around to this approach "not always wholeheartedly and often only partially," as Dutch media historian Marcel Broersma has put it.[10]

It was only in the mid-twentieth century that continental newspapers began to use headlines. Newspapers before that time and some even after World War II employed what Broersma calls a "vertical" layout – there was a standard order of domains of news (national news, foreign, local), one story separated from the next by a short line, and if there were headlines at all, they were categorical rather than substantive: "The War" or "The Paris Conference." There was no way that, at a glance, a reader could judge what news the news organization thought the most important. There was no editorial judgment being exercised and, again in Broersma's words, "journalists often did not extract the news from an event."[11] European journalists to some degree stuck to their "expressive" or "reflective" rather than reportorial style of work. In one last quotation from Broersma, "European journalism largely remained more centered on the exposition of ideas than straightforward reporting of bare facts."[12]

The professional ideal that casts reporting the story as the heart of journalism is not fully accepted everywhere, but I think it has a strong foothold in most parts of the world, even in countries where news organizations strain against state censorship. Professionalism in journalism consists in knowing what "news" is and how to locate it, how to verify it, and how to present it. For journalists to take into account considerations of other matters – whether social justice or community pride or national security – is, at best, uncomfortable in the eyes of journalists, and borders on serious corruption. By what authority are journalists, who may indeed be skillful at determining what news is, accorded the right to make consequential judgments about what counts as social justice or what information should be withheld on the grounds of national security? Does this not, in journalists' own eyes, pollute the purely journalistic task? And yet some of these impurities are everyday occurrences among the best news organizations and others are occasional occurrences that indicate how difficult it is for journalists to stick to their "DNA" like a monk or a nun to their vows.

What Kind of Journalism Matters Most?

The everyday deviation from the pure reportorial fact-collecting task of journalism is that journalists write as well as report and that what they seek to write is a "story," which is a form that at its best seeks to touch a reader or viewer; it does not aim only to transmit information. This seems obvious – that journalists should keep their audience in mind – but once this is allowed, then the entire yawning gulf of the role of the marketplace in shaping news presents itself, not to mention subjective judgments about what is or is not a report in the public interest. At a minimum, writing stories means that journalists regularly seek to connect emotionally with their audiences. Media scholar Karin Wahl-Jorgensen has shown that in the US journalists are more likely to win Pulitzer prizes if they convey emotion in the news they report. They portray the human beings they write about as emotional creatures, often caught in a moment of crisis and riven or elevated by intense feelings – of sorrow or triumph, of despair or hope, of joy or anger. These are the features that enable "information" to come alive and touch the audience.[13]

Telling stories is what journalists do. And telling stories is not reciting a list of facts but putting reported facts together in a way that might touch a reader or viewer. Committees awarding prizes for journalistic achievement recognize this and reward it. The textbooks journalism students study in their classes make the same point. Al Tompkins, prize-winning journalist and later journalism trainer at the influential Poynter Institute in St. Petersburg, Florida, wrote a text entitled, *Aim for the Heart* – exactly Wahl-Jorgensen's point. And Tompkins, with a wide variety of examples from his own and others' experience in newsrooms, offers advice on how to reach the hearts of viewers, listeners, and readers.[14]

The more unusual occurrences that violate journalistic DNA are, although rare, very telling. In 2003, Dean Baquet, today the executive editor of the *New York Times* but then the managing editor of the *Los Angeles Times*, oversaw a newsroom that had come up with a damaging story about Arnold Schwarzenegger, the well-known Hollywood actor who was then a leading candidate for governor of California. A half-dozen women in the movie industry had made credible allegations that Schwarzenegger had sexually harassed them. The story was ready to go just days before the election, but editors wondered if they should delay publishing until after the vote. It was so close to polling day, would it not seem to be a kind of last-minute "hit piece" sprung on Schwarzenegger, giving him too little time to respond?

The *Times* went ahead to publish. Nevertheless, Schwarzenegger went on to win the election resoundingly. Later, Baquet told a reporter writing a post-mortem about the Schwarzenegger sexual harassment news coverage, "Sometimes people don't understand that to not publish is a big decision for a newspaper and almost a political act. That's not an act of journalism. You're letting your decision-making get clouded by things that have nothing to do with what a newspaper is supposed to do."[15] Journalists publish, in Baquet's view, full stop. Insufficient quality of the journalism would be a reason to not publish. The possibility that publishing could endanger a life would be a reason to withhold a story that met all the standards of good journalism. But, for Baquet, that was about it. Any other reason to not publish is not a good one.

More than a decade later, Baquet would adjust his formulation. In 2016, he was the executive editor of the *New York Times*, and under the weight of decisions that fell in large part to him as the chief of the news operation of the world's most influential newspaper concerning whether to publish the massive disclosures of US state secrets provided by WikiLeaks, then Chelsea Manning, then Edward Snowden. And if so, how, and how much? He explained his views in an interview with the BBC. He declared that the early WikiLeaks "data dumps" provided important information to the global public, but he felt much more ambivalent about more recent disclosures. The early disclosure

> was clearly journalistically newsworthy. It seemed that the source was idealistic. But we're now in an era when governments are weaponizing hacking. But I still think, even though it makes me queasy, that if someone gives us information that's really important and vital for people to know, we've gotta figure out a way to publish it – even if the source is part of the story.

He told the BBC that he would have published some – but not all – of the material that in the end only Buzzfeed published: the "dossier" on Donald Trump's relations with the Russians prepared by a respected former British intelligence officer, Christopher Steele. But, he made clear, he would have published only the information that seemed to be publicly significant, and he would do so only by being transparent about the sources of the information and what could be gleaned about their motives, and he would not consider the public figures' private lives to be publicly important.[16]

I mention Baquet's somewhat meandering remarks and apparent departure from his 2003 "journalists publish" orthodoxy not to criticize a distinguished journalist but to indicate how deeply the new information environment of our own digital and global era complicates fundamental features of journalism. Inventing a philosophy of journalism on the fly – and with the entire globe looking on – is not an enviable task. So we can observe the improvised character of Baquet's thinking over time, but just what would I do in Baquet's seat? What would you do?

Where Baquet has been consistent, from Arnold Schwarzenegger in 2003 to drone warfare in 2015, is in holding fast to a distinction between journalism and politics. In a 2015 interview with Harvard Law School professor Jack Goldsmith, he practically quoted himself from 2003 – ". . . to not publish, in my way of thinking, is almost a political act. To not publish is a big deal." And so, he explained to Goldsmith, in the tricky business of publishing or not publishing state secrets, he pushes espionage agencies or other agencies to persuade him to not publish when they ask him to not publish: "Guys, make the case. You can't just say that it hurts national security. You can't just say vaguely that it's going to get somebody killed. You've got to help me, tell me." He still sometimes decides to not publish, but only when the government officials have persuaded him that the lives of US soldiers or US spies or allies, would really be put at risk if the *Times* published the story it was sitting on.[17]

It did not require the Internet or vast leaks of data for key news organizations to develop extraordinary procedures for consulting with the US government when they had a story that might affect national security. For at least half a century, leading news organizations have on occasions set aside the usual presumption that the journalist's obligation is to publish well-documented stories on topics of public importance. Such judgments have been made at least as far back as 1961 when the *New York Times* got wind of the impending US-supported invasion of Fidel Castro's Cuba at the Bay of Pigs, and it let the government know and voluntarily modified its story on the strenuous urgings of the White House. It was again the case a generation later when in 1986 the *Washington Post* learned of a secret US underwater mechanism code-named "Ivy Bells" that tapped Soviet cable communications but that had been compromised by a low-level technician for the National Security Agency, Jack Pelton. Pelton sold his information about Ivy Bells to the Russians. *Post* newsroom executives met with NSA Director Lieutenant General William Odom, who urged them not to publish anything – it would endanger the country, revealing to the Soviets something they did not know. But they already know, editor Ben Bradlee countered. No, Odom said, that was not clear – which Soviets? There may have been internal Soviet secrecy or cover-up, but a story in the *Post* would set off a general alarm in the Soviet Union and increase Soviet anti-espionage measures. This made the *Post* cautious. *Post* editors and reporters worked on successive drafts of the story, each providing less detail than the one before. Bradlee repeatedly asked, "What social purpose is there in this story?" In the end, the *Post* published over the objections of the administration – in a negotiation that dragged out over five months.[18]

In these cases, the US press reluctantly took on a sense of stewardship in the public interest or a co-guardianship with the government for the public good – understood as the national good of the US. When reporters Eric Lichtblau and Jim Risen learned that American intelligence agencies were illegally doing surveillance on the telephone calls of American citizens, they held the story for a year – and regretted doing so. Often, as *New York Times*' legal counsel David McCraw has written, the paper has decided that "the government's objections were too abstract, not believable, insufficiently weighty, or given by officials too far down the food chain to know, and our editors have then resolved to move ahead with publishing. But it's not a science. Editors sometimes get it wrong. National security is intrinsically the hardest of the calls they have to make."[19]

Even in normal, daily journalism, values other than "get the facts, get the story" enter in. A special case is that of the BBC, nationally chartered by the British government to provide service to the British nation. The BBC acknowledges an obligation to serve needs of national identity. At its beginning, it was self-consciously dedicated to promoting a sense of Britishness that included celebrating what it took to be a distinctively British heritage, including, even, allegiance to the practices of the Church of England. This was a matter not of considering national security but of embracing the forging of national identity as an organizational goal.

If something like the BBC's allegiance to a goal of national unity would be questioned by the creeds of American journalism, is there, nevertheless, an informal moral agenda American journalists subscribe to? In 1970 US journalist Jack Newfield wrote disapprovingly that there was – that most American journalists share a "belief in welfare capitalism, God, the West, Puritanism, the Law, the family, property, the two-party system, and perhaps most crucially, in the notion that violence is only defensible when employed by the State."[20] In the ensuing half-century, "God" has mostly dropped out, "Puritanism" certainly has, and there have been modifications to most of the other values on Newfield's list. More systematically, sociologist Herbert Gans held that American journalists hold some "enduring values" they may not even be aware that they share. Gans's list of enduring values includes ethnocentrism (that it is appropriate to write far more about the US than about the rest of the world), "responsible capitalism" (that capitalism is our perfectly acceptable economic system but that capitalist institutions should be "responsible" in considering – besides profit – the public good), "altruistic democracy," and "moderatism" (that extreme positions to the right and left of a political center are to be distrusted and perhaps do not even merit mention because political truth typically lies somewhere in the middle).[21] Gans arrived at his list in 1979 and it still holds up pretty well as a description of underlying normative positions in the newsrooms of the mainstream media. It suggests not a bias in the sense of a design or intention to slant the news but a bias of background, unconsidered or barely considered assumptions about what is good and bad, right and wrong about the contemporary world and its chief institutions, and thereby what to recognize as deviations or departures from normal behavior and normal practices that might either call out as "news" (the way a murder does) or cry out "I am beyond the acceptable limits of topics worthy of public discourse."

These are the sorts of values that creep into journalism unbidden and unconsciously but frequently. The national security consultations with the government crash in more rarely, and do not receive a warm welcome. After all, they push journalism beyond its comfort zone – holding the powerful government accountable – and into its danger zone: acting almost as if it were a part of the government itself.

When journalism operates in its comfort zone, it honors an ideal of professional journalism that is all about holding the powerful accountable – what former *Washington Post* executive editor Leonard Downie, Jr. terms "accountability journalism." By that he means "traditional investigative reporting but much more" – he also includes fact-checking political speeches and aggressive everyday coverage of various news beats from national security to government, politics, business, the environment, education, and the news media industry itself.[22]

And what exactly is accountability journalism at its best? It is a journalism of original reporting, presented in an emotionally compelling way, and asserting itself in the face of the powerful persons and institutions it covers – all in the interest of helping make a democratic government more fully accountable to the public.

Democracy cannot truly exist if accountability journalism does not. But journalism of some sort certainly exists where democracy does not. Journalists in non-democracies may aspire to something like the professionalism of journalists in democratic countries, but their aspirations cannot be fully satisfied. There are degrees of repression of journalistic inquiry; degrees of access the powerful permit journalists; degrees of coercion from insult and harassment up to and including threat, assault, imprisonment, and murder. There are dictatorships that straightforwardly oppose free speech and a free press and there are "illiberal democracies" where elected leaders target independent media for attack. Both the dictatorships and the illiberal autocrats tolerate a journalism that is still journalism, but it is largely toothless, not a different form of journalism so much as a sickly and wounded form of a standard professional journalism.

There are other wounded and wounding journalisms, too. An argument for the best professional journalism does not deny that much harm comes from the worst that journalism peddles. Tabloid journalism or entertainment journalism can be enjoyable for millions, but in its efforts to scandalize, to make mountains of molehills, to lie or mislead for the sake of sensation – "Martians sighted in Alaska!" – it causes two sorts of harm. First, it distracts people's limited attention from genuine and genuinely important news. Second, when it produces almost irresistibly shareable items, they then get widely recirculated online. A recent British study surveyed people who share political news on Twitter. It found that "UK tabloid newspapers negatively affect the quality of civic life on social media" because those surveyed acknowledged that they share information online they suspect to be false or even know to be false.[23] Here old-fashioned scurrilous journalism conspires with new online opportunities for extending its reach and polluting civic space.

3

Reported, Compelling, and Assertive: Anatomy of Journalism That Matters

For an academic to call a piece of writing "journalistic" is invariably to discredit it. This is true in the US. It is equally true in France: "If a French professor writes in the margin of a student's essay 'journalistique' . . . it means not deep enough, full of clichés. There is no need to say that 'trés universitaire' (very academic) is not a compliment when used in a newsroom."[1] Let's be honest here, speaking as the academic I am: sometimes journalism is deeper and richer than all but the finest and rarest scholarship in the humanities and social sciences. The only thing that almost invariably distinguishes scholarship from journalism is that the measure of its excellence is whether it contributes something new to "the literature."[2] This means it should be addressed to ongoing debates, controversies, or open questions among experts in the field. If it is very successful, it adds something so novel or criticizes prior work so decisively that it overturns past verities and changes the direction of thinking in the area. Academic work is addressed to a long conversation going back at least a few years, often a decade or two, and sometimes centuries. What journalism generally intends is a conversation about the new for the now. It is of and for the moment, although its impact may on occasion be widespread and long-lasting.

"News" is as old as the hills but journalism is a distinctly modern invention, arising in the West in the 1500s and 1600s and reaching considerable prominence by the mid-1800s. Even so, as I have already touched on, most newspapers were miscellanies, one paper reprinting stories lifted from another, running random contributions from readers themselves, and running pieces authored by government bureaus, random travelers, commercial notices (ads), regular correspondents – paid or unpaid, poems, explicitly fictional works, and much more. The news page or pages were likely to reflect the order in which stories came to the newspaper office and the ways by which they came. ("News by Telegraph" was a familiar headline under which a set of separate stories was printed whose connecting feature was that all had come to the paper by telegraph.) Only in the twentieth century did journalism's growing occupational self-consciousness acquire elements of a professional pride and a set of moral rules or patterns about what a reporter should do – in relation to accuracy, fairness, neutrality or what would be called by the 1920s "objectivity."

Again, there are multiple journalisms. Even within the professional journalism I focus on here, there are multiple variants. There are forms of journalism that – often at some remove from immediate events or issues and often finding an outlet in books or in magazines but also in daily newspapers – focus on telling their audience something about its neighbors or about people in other societies and other nations, not in the form of travelogues, but in an effort to help that audience understand other ways of life and other points of view. This is a journalism of social empathy – terribly important, in my judgment, but normally not the first thing people think of when reflecting on "why journalism matters." There is also a journalism of critical reflection: expert responses to things new wherever they are – a new court decision, a new law, a new movie or play or scientific discovery or piece of music or new performance of an old piece of music. All of this – all of it called "journalism" – plays a role in building a public and a public conversation that helps make a society possible.

The beating heart of journalism is an effort to relate to a public what political leaders have done, what they are doing, and what they intend to do. Journalism monitors the work of elected and appointed public servants and turns its searchlight on the achievements and the failures and the corruptions of these men and women in public office. Some related work may be done by opposition parties. Some related work may be done by other associations in civil society. But no other institution does this work so consistently and with such independence of mind as the professional press, and that, in a nutshell, is why journalism matters.

Despite the economic woes of journalism (when will we find the next "business model"?), notwithstanding the significant competition from non-professional producers of news that has grown greatly with the amateur's ubiquitous presence, with a cellphone camera, at news events where no professional journalist happened to be present, and in the face of declining levels of public trust in "the media" (though how people understand the vague terms "trust' and "the media" is unclear), professionally produced journalism is very likely better than it has ever been.

Reported, Compelling, and Assertive

But what does "better" mean for the journalism that matters most? What characterizes journalism that holds the powerful accountable to the public and to the institutions of a democracy? Fundamentally, it is journalism that is ably reported, emotionally compelling, and assertive in standing up to power. I will discuss each of these criteria in turn.

Reported

Fundamental competence in original journalism means doing the reporting to get the relevant facts and to get them right. It is about not making up anything but trusting – within reason and with an appropriate level of skepticism for detecting baloney and bullshit – that people you interview will be relatively honest (or their dishonesty will be apparent), that documents you examine will have been created to be useful for a variety of internal purposes, and that that means, depending on the organization and its purposes, that the document was intended to communicate something accurately and can be – within reason, again, and with appropriate skepticism – trusted. For many stories much of the time, the judgment calls about the reliability of evidence are not complicated. For some stories some of the time, they could scarcely be more difficult.

Doing the reporting means being able to assess the reliability of evidence. It also means knowing when you have come upon something that might be widely judged to be "news." If anything is the heart of the matter of what makes a journalist, this is it, a "nose for news." British scholar Stuart Hall found fifty years ago "news values" or a "news sense" to be among "the most opaque structures of meaning in modern society. All 'true journalists' are supposed to possess it: few can or are willing to identify and define it." And American sociologist Gaye Tuchman wrote at the same time that "news judgment is the sacred knowledge, the secret ability of the newsman which differentiates him from other people."[3] Reporting is knowing how to pursue verification of what you have been told or what you think you have found. Reporting is putting facts together into a coherent story. Reporting – but this goes beyond the gathering of information that will be the basis of the report – is writing a story that is compelling.

Compelling

I don't know any journalists who think their work should be about the facts, the facts, and only the facts. They are all trying to communicate more than cold, easily forgettable true things. At a symposium on covering climate change at the Columbia Journalism School on April 30, 2019, Soomini Sengupta of the *New York Times* said her team of reporters try to make the coverage "compelling, rich, personal." She felt that they had a mission "to move people," allowing them to feel "the human toll of climate change." The difficult task in covering a slow-moving disaster like this one, Sengupta said, is "to make it matter to our four million subscribers." A day later, on another panel, Richard Webster, a reporter at NOLA.com in New Orleans, accepted a Dart Center for Journalism and Trauma prize as part of a team covering a group of young people in a crime-ridden, drug-ridden, and notably murder-ridden neighborhood of the city. He defined "great stories" as "the ones that enable the story to make an emotional connection to readers."

Why, asked two Swedish scholars in 1970, are news stories so often "personified"? Is this a liberal, Western, individual-centered bias? That is, does it stem from norms and values specific to some societies? Or could it be something about the nature of story-telling itself across societies, connected to a need in narratives to connect with the audience and establish "identification"?[4] Or could it be – a possibility they did not consider – that it had to do with reporters' need for verification? If journalists can point to individuals who said something or did something specific at a given time and place that can be confirmed by observation, testimony, or documents, they are on firm, defensible ground. If they focus on underlying structures or long-term processes rather than individual actions, they shift the weight of the story to interpretation and analysis. This will raise questions – either from an editor or from the audience. It may be some combination of these factors, but surely "personification" is one of those features of many (by no means all) news stories that enables audiences to become emotionally engaged by them.

When journalists defend their journalism against critics, they talk about reporting. When they explain what they are trying to do in their work, they talk about story-telling. Defensively, they emphasize facts. In terms of their relationship to an audience, they stress stories, meaning-making, feeling. Both the insistent, even obsessive attention to factual details and the effort to string the details together into an emotionally compelling story must be understood to comprehend what journalism is and what makes it work – when it does.[5]

Former *Chicago Tribune* editor Jack Fuller bravely recommended that serious journalists look to tabloid or down-market newspapers and even tabloid television for ideas on how to gain and keep the attention of audiences. Without neglecting the significant social and civic missions of journalism, he writes, how can responsible journalists use suspense to advance them? How can they use celebrity to "draw attention to problems of genuine importance," and how can they harness "the personality of the presenter," the way tabloid rhetoric often does, to serve a broad public mission?[6]

Assertive

Consider the quandary of Afghan journalists in Afghanistan. Without a native tradition of journalism, they have learned their journalism from the West. As one Afghan reporter told researcher Katherine Brown, the American reporters "inspired us with their audacity for questioning people." That went against the grain of traditional Afghan culture. As one US journalist in Afghanistan put it,

44

"It's in Afghan culture that you don't put people on the spot."[7]

A taboo against discrediting one's elders has been common among the world's cultures, if not practically universal, and it has certainly been an influence in the development of even British and American journalism. As noted in the previous chapter, when American reporters began in the late nineteenth century to directly ask questions of both politicians and celebrities, European journalists found this a crude (but typically American) practice they were unwilling to countenance – but later adopted.

Interviewing is one form of assertiveness that has been accepted by reporters around the world – although it remains more difficult in some societies than in others. Investigative reporting is an assertiveness far more aggressive, if less widely practiced. In South America, investigative journalism was not widely adopted until the 1980s and 1990s. Until then, the region's journalism had "systematically shunned critical reporting and opted for complacent relations with state and market interests." It was hard to find anything one could name "watchdog reporting" in mainstream journalism until then. But watchdog reporting, under the inspiration of US journalism and sometimes under American tutelage, went mainstream in the 1980s and 1990s.

When media scholar Silvio Waisbord wrote about this in the late 1990s, he was unwilling to predict "whether this is a passing fad or will become a regular part of the press in the region,"[8] but today he finds that it has indeed become a regular part of the press.

What is new is that some of the leading practitioners of investigative reporting work for online sites. There are at least a dozen online news organizations in Latin America that "have regularly produced well-researched investigations." These sites include organizations in Mexico, Peru, Guatemala, and Colombia. Most of these would not have launched without international aid and philanthropy, notably including the Open Society Foundations. Like others in North America and Europe, these organizations struggle to diversify their business models.[9]

We might distinguish three general forms of assertive reporting. One is face-to-face reporting when journalists meet directly with government officials, especially in publicly videotaped or even live broadcast settings. This does not have to be assertive and, in both Britain and the United States, in the early years of various forms of televised press conferences, reporters asked only the most deferential questions and rarely followed up questions that the government official had not fully or adequately or honestly answered. But over time, as elegantly conducted research by sociolinguists has demonstrated, reporters grew routinely more aggressive in their questions and in following up one question with a second or third more insistent question on the same topic.[10]

Second, there is investigative reporting – the most expensive form of assertiveness, the most time-consuming, and the least certain to pay off with significant news. Its expense makes it the least common form of assertiveness. Most news organizations do little or no investigative work. And its assertiveness is also a strike against it; the idea – and partial fiction – that journalists cover the news and do not become part of it is hard to maintain when the news organization makes a decision to invest in a long-term investigative effort. If it is an effort that follows up a specific news event, that is relatively straightforward (but still expensive). But when it is an effort to investigate a topic that does not specifically respond to a breaking news event, then that is more obviously an intervention in the public agenda rather than an exploration of an established public agenda. What is encouraging in this regard, in the digital era, is that a number of online news operations are dedicated primarily to investigative reporting – it is not simply a sideline of a more general news-gathering effort.

Third, there is analytical reporting that enters into or accompanies or quickly follows a straight news story. Increasingly, since roughly 1970, US news organizations have broken away from the "he said/she said" kind of report in which the writer quotes a leader of one major party and quotes a rejoinder from a representative of a major rival, or quotes the leader of the government coalition and then a rejoinder from the leader of the parliamentary opposition, and calls it a day. In the 1960s, as critics of standard routines of "objectivity" became more and more vocal – and more and more convincing – it became more widely accepted that "objectivity" had become a crutch rather than a code of good conduct. In an effort to keep the reporter from voicing his or her own judgment, it allowed government officials to dominate the news. Analysis – the provision of context to make a current debate or disagreement meaningful to the audience – is inevitable if news reports are to be understood. Newspapers have increasingly accepted analytical reporting or contextual reporting as essential and worthy of front-page prominence.[11]

Journalism of the 1950s or 1960s was not the good old days. Journalism was then too tame and too smug, too likely to see itself as appropriately part of the king's court, the inner circle of political power. The past fifty years have founded a deeper professionalism than then existed, a firmer commitment to accountability, and a journalism that, at its best, is one of the political and cultural treasures of our time.

4

The Problem of Media Bias

An ironic triumph of professional journalism is
that practically everyone is eager to demonstrate
their sophistication by pointing out that the news
is biased.

It is a first sign of wisdom to realize no one is
without a perspective, a stance, a position from
which they view the world. There is no "objective"
or neutral perspective on reality.

Is every perspective partial? Of course it is. That's
why there are systems of education and training to
supplement and indeed to supplant native perspectives with trained perceptions. Medical school, law
school, engineering school, and others seek to instill
in students not only mastery of a body of knowledge and mastery of specific techniques of practice
but also a re-education of the students' instincts
for approaching the world. They seek to replace

personal reflex with professional judgment when it comes to doing the work they are being trained to take on. That is why the American Medical Association urges surgeons not to operate on their own family members, where personal affections would be especially likely to cloud professional judgment.

No doctor, no lawyer, no engineer, no scientist, and no trained journalist would ever deny that some judgments are better than others, more true than others, more faithful to accepted evidence and criteria for evidence. To be fair to skeptics, journalism is not as sophisticated a field as medicine. It has almost no technical terminology. Training takes one or two years of study – or no formal study at all – compared to a college degree plus roughly four years of medical school and roughly four more years in internships and residencies to produce a fully educated physician. But the less rigorous training in journalism is training, nonetheless. And, like medicine, it is training in ethics as well as in techniques. Becoming a professional is learning how to place professional judgment above personal tastes and inclinations.

My colleagues who teach beginning journalism students say that they are intent on helping them learn to "report against their own assumptions."

That is, whatever inclinations or presuppositions the students bring to a story, they should go about their research with inquiries that potentially call into question exactly those inclinations and presuppositions. They are instructed against "confirmation bias": that is, looking for just those people to interview or those documents to gather that would most likely confirm the views they brought to the story in the first place. My journalist colleague Jelani Cobb of the *New Yorker*, speaking to my class of undergraduate students, recommended that those seeking a career in journalism should follow two reporting rules: first, dig in and find out everything they can on their subject; and, second, forget prior knowledge, because it can get in the way of what they will learn. Is there a well-developed set of techniques or practices that would accomplish this? No, it is more of an ethic and an insistent aspiration than it is a set of methods.

If young journalists do not learn these lessons well in school, they will pick them up, perhaps painfully, in the newsroom. Sam Freedman, a faculty colleague at the Columbia Journalism School, recalls that, as a fledgling reporter at the *New York Times*, he came back from covering a controversial referendum in a Connecticut town, proudly turned in his story, and then heard the icy response of his editor, Jeff Schmalz. "When I read this story, I know exactly what Sam Freedman thinks." The assignment, as Schmalz then made very clear, was to report about a referendum in a Connecticut town and not to report about the journalist's opinions. Sam would "rewrite as quickly as possible" to regain his editor's approval. The reporter was being paid not for his views but for his reporting.[1]

Non-professionals also find ways to separate their judgments from their preferences. In English, there is a common phrase, "If I were in your shoes . . .," to introduce advice that a teacher might offer a student, a friend might offer a friend, a parent might offer a grown child. "If I were in your shoes . . ." is an effort to say, "I am not in your shoes and I know you are different from me and I do not know exactly how the world looks from where you stand, but as best as I can imagine your standpoint and as well as I can imagine what's best for you, here's what I think." "If I were in your shoes . . ." is a kind of thought-experiment to make a more objective judgment rather than simply to impose my values on you.

That is the sort of thing professionals are expected to learn. Do they ever put their own values entirely aside? No. But can they make concerted and con-sequential efforts to do so? They can and often they do. And it seems to me wildly naïve to assume that "bias" inevitably overwhelms self-restraining efforts of this sort.

There is such a thing as trying to get outside oneself. There is such a thing as empathy. There is such a thing as human curiosity. There is such a thing as wanting to give others a fair shake. The reflex to say "the media are biased" seeks to sound deep ("I can recognize bias") but it often ends up superficial.

And it's well to remember what researchers call the "hostile media effect." The more engaged and the more polarized audiences are, the more likely they will perceive "the media" to be hostile to their own position. "It is what audiences do with news, as well as what newspeople do with news, that accounts for judgments of trust in mass media."[2] The more engaged you are in polarized politics, the more you are likely to know about the issues, but also the more you are likely to be indignant about any reporting you think gives the other side more of a voice or a more sympathetic hearing than you think is merited.

I was reminded of this "hostile media effect" recently when I met with an old friend, a long-time civil liberties activist, who turned to me as a "media expert" in hopes I would confirm his view that the *New York Times* was strongly pro-Trump. Pro-

Trump? I cited several recent stories in the paper that took on recent Trump statements and demonstrated decisively that he spoke nonsense. The *Times* indicated – as it now does routinely – that Mr. Trump simply has no regard for factual truth. My friend, however, was convinced that the paper was in Trump's pocket.

Of course, journalism is rarely a matter of isolated individuals, each seeking to discipline himself or herself to put professional norms above personal preferences. Most journalists work for or in relationship to news organizations, some of them large and powerful, and these news organizations have instituted practices and ideals designed to minimize certain kinds of bias. Do news organizations always reproduce in their news content what the owner of the news organization would wish them to produce? No. The owner is supposed to keep his or her busybody instincts in check and stay the hell out of the newsroom. A liberal like Jeff Bezos seems to be doing a good job of this at the *Washington Post*. And while conservative Rupert Murdoch has been perfectly willing to select executive editors for the news organizations he owns who will be guided by his own political views, at least in the case of the *Wall Street Journal* and London's *Times*, he recognizes that the value of these properties will decline sharply if he violates the autonomy of the newsroom. In a striking account, *Wall Street Journal* reporter John Carreyrou reveals how Elizabeth Holmes, the charismatic CEO of Theranos, a medical-testing Silicon Valley start-up, met personally with Murdoch to ask him to intervene to kill a devastatingly critical story that Carreyrou had written about the company. She had reason to think he would be responsive to her plea – after all, he had recently invested $150 million in Theranos himself. But Murdoch "declined to intervene." The news staff made its own decisions, published the story, and sealed the fate of the company.[3]

Within the daily operation of news organizations, there is a "business side" and a "news side," and here, too, there is a self-denying ordinance in operation: the business side, like the owner, is supposed to stay the hell out of the newsroom. This was never perfectly achieved, but the gulf between "news" and "business" has been bridged more often in the past decade in the US as leading news organizations have lent their skills to advertisers or potential advertisers to write ads – "native advertising" – that intentionally and deceptively read like news stories.

In recent decades, news organizations have grown sensitive to some of their own practices they were once blind to, seeking greater diversity of standpoint by making efforts to hire (and promote) minorities and women in what were, within living memory, overwhelmingly white and male newsroom populations. Sexism and racism in mainstream newsrooms were taken for granted into the 1970s. When reporter Meg Greenfield came to the US capital as Washington correspondent for a national magazine in 1961, a male colleague took her to the National Press Club, where they both discovered what her male colleague had never noticed before: women journalists were not permitted to enter except for certain special social occasions.[4] They would not be allowed membership until 1971. In 1970 (although they were labeled "researchers" rather than reporters and were denied the opportunity to apply for reporter positions) *Newsweek*'s women journalists filed a suit for discrimination against them in hiring and promotion. They hired a young African-American attorney, Eleanor Holmes Norton, later to be a famous civil rights advocate and a member of Congress. The suit was successful and path-breaking, the first sex discrimination suit in the US media industry, and an experience that, in the words of participant Lynn Povich, who later wrote a book about it, "changed our perspectives about ourselves, about men and women – and womanhood – and about justice and ambition."[5] In that book, lawyer Norton reports that she regretted that she did not ask the black women researchers to join the lawsuit – nor, it seems, had that occurred to the white women who initiated it.[6]

There is no bias-free journalism, nor will there ever be. The initial suit and a follow-up suit at *Newsweek* opened full-fledged careers in journalism to women at the magazine for the first time, but that was just one notable step on a long trek for gender equality that continues in media organizations and society at large. This brief chapter is not intended to deny that there is bias in news organizations and in news content, including at the best, most professional, most dedicated news operations. Instead, I hope simply to remind journalism consumers and journalism critics that professional journalism insists on practices of evidence-gathering that give a voice to different viewpoints, and it calls for reporters and editors to hold their own values and preferences in check while dedicating themselves to follow the story.

Professional journalists are not all about insinuating their own politics or religion into their work but about doing their work seriously, informing their audience about the changing world, with all of its complexity, and how it has shifted in recent days or hours. That's their job. That's what they try to do.

5

Evidence That Journalism Matters (or Doesn't)

There are few things more difficult in the social sciences than trying to pinpoint the influence of the mass media. We can measure the reach of media messages – in imperfect ways, to be sure, but in ways there is good reason to find roughly reliable.

But this is only the beginning of trying to figure out if a message in the news influences the people it reaches. We know that there is a very high "correlation" between voting Republican and watching Fox News in the United States. But why? Is it that (1) Republicans gravitate to Fox News, knowing full well it will reinforce their conservative inclinations? Or is it that (2) Fox News convinces otherwise independent or Democratic voters to become more conservative? Explanation (1) is certainly correct – people regularly search for information that will reinforce the views they already hold –

but explanation (2) could be part of the answer, too. Some people come to Fox News accidentally. Perhaps they are in a hotel lobby or a bus terminal and Fox News is on the screen. Or maybe they are just channel-surfing at home and there is something especially eye-catching on Fox that stops them for a few minutes. In this case, Fox virgins might be seduced. Or surely some regular Fox viewers, of centrist or liberal political views, stay loyal to Fox because they find it entertaining. And Fox must reach some only moderately politicized people who don't often think about politics and don't have views about most public issues and who therefore may be easily persuadable.

We do not know the degree to which the second possibility – persuasion – mixes with the first – reinforcement and reassurance. But nearly a century of research in psychology and social psychology shows, as Kenneth Newton has summarized it, that "individuals are able to ignore, suppress, misinterpret, forget, misremember, misunderstand, avoid, or deny information and opinion that does not accord with their own view of the world."[1]

Many people believe that the advent of cable television in the United States, bringing with it highly partisan channels – notably Fox (for conservatives) and MSNBC (for liberals) – helped polarize American public life. Perhaps. But the best evidence so far seems to be that, in both Britain and the United States, there is notable polarization of national politics while only very small segments of the population on the far right and the far left wrap themselves exclusively in a small set of news sources that reinforce their extreme views. In general, the largest effect of cable television on politics in the US has been that millions of people have fled from television news altogether, preferring to spend their time on specialized sports channels or home shopping networks, or other entertainment channels far from "news."[2]

The ordinary person may believe that businesses advertise because they know that advertising works, but the truth is that they advertise because they know that advertising *might* work. Even a successful advertising campaign may lead only three or four people out of 100 exposed to it to buy a product they had not previously intended to buy. That may be enough to justify the advertising expense, but, if so, this is a case where influencing four people in 100 is called success. Is the non-influence on the other 96 people a failure? There is an old saying in advertising: "I know half of my advertising dollars are wasted; I just don't know which half!"

In some obvious ways, the media have limited

power over audiences because they have no leverage over them, only a communicative link to them. In contrast, a parent can chastise a child who does not comply with parental directives; a teacher can give a student a poor grade; a military officer can punish a subordinate with everything from public humiliation to referral to the military judicial system; a bureaucrat can assign a dissenting or disruptive subordinate to the least desirable tasks or threaten to delay or deny advancement. But what can the BBC or Reuters or NHK or *Le Monde* or the *Wall Street Journal* do to their audiences? Nothing at all. They trade only in symbols – words and pictures – and their audiences can take them or leave them.

So even when the media raise questions of public policy, it is not easy to know how to evaluate their impact. Do warning labels on cigarette packages help reduce smoking? Should comic books have been banned (there were efforts to do so) because they corrupted youth? Do video games corrupt youth? Should pornography be banned for the harm it presumably causes? Will anything I write in this little book have any short-term or long-term influence on anyone? If so, will it be the influence I intended or something else? It is a long road from a media message reaching someone to its influencing how that person thinks or acts. Does the message shape what a person thinks? Or perhaps only what that person *momentarily* thinks about? Or does it simply sensitize the person to what other people may be thinking or thinking about?

For those of us absorbed in the seemingly endless and countless discussions and debates about the news media, it is sobering to browse through general history books where journalism is hardly ever mentioned and never becomes a major topic. The Great Forces of history are typically politicians, social movements, technological changes, economic ups and downs, occasionally some bold new idea that catches on: say, Keynesian economics or the Gandhian idea of *satyagraha* that helped organized the Indian resistance to British colonial rule. But "the media" as a social force? It rarely appears, even in history textbooks of 500 or 600 pages.

So do we have evidence that journalism matters – that it has some notable impact on the world?

Yes, we do. But we have never had a systematic and comprehensive accounting of it. In fact, my own sense is that "a systematic accounting" is not conceivable because some of the most important effects of journalism are simply not open to quantification. Media may structure people's use of their time. Media may shape atmosphere. But such media influence is not very often a matter of "the news media reported such-and-such and therefore so-and-so occurred." Even so, we can enumerate a set of recognizable types of influence of journalism – types that anyone reading this book already knows about but may never have put into words. What we cannot do and will not ever be able to do is to devise some summary measure that adds them all up. If you have two apples and three oranges and a broiled fish and a baked potato, how much dining satisfaction do you have? Yes, you could count the calories and figure out how much nutrition is on offer, but how much that influences the diner's level of happiness is something else entirely. These are quite different sorts of influence, each of them hard to measure and none of them measurable on a common scale that could link them together to construct a single, general index of food influence.

So what are the varieties of media influence? Let me suggest three key types of influence. The news media: (1) help people know where they stand in the world; (2) provide relevant new information; and (3) hold powerful institutions and individuals accountable.

Evidence That Journalism Matters (or Doesn't)

Knowing Where We Are – Flagging and Naming Contemporary Currents

It seems to me very likely that the most important "effect" of journalism is one that no one has tried to measure but that Hannah Arendt had the wisdom to identify when she wrote that without journalists "we should never find our bearings in an ever-changing world and, in the most literal sense, would never know where we are."[3] I have read Arendt's famous essay "Truth and Politics" multiple times and never stopped on that passage until I came upon it recently cited in Natalia Roudakova's book on the Soviet and post-Soviet press. Roudakova saw, as I had not, that this is an exact and indispensable insight, almost too obvious to have gained notice. But maybe I can illustrate it in a way to help give it a shape. Journalism captures the evanescent but recognizably important in human affairs that we had no name for until journalists provided it. Novelists and film-makers and others with special sensitivity to the flux and flow of contemporary affairs, styles, moods, trends just below the surface and just before a moment of clear articulation share this role with journalists, but this does not diminish the role of journalism in this pursuit.

Sometimes journalism can change thinking in the wider world by efficiently and memorably naming something that everybody already knows or senses but has not quite been able to grasp. For instance, consider the word "mansplaining." The phenomenon was first isolated as a "thing" to write about and to criticize by the writer-journalist-thinker Rebecca Solnit in an online 2008 essay, "Men Explain Things To Me." The term, as such, apparently first appeared in a comment on "LiveJournal" a month later. By 2010 it was selected by the *New York Times* as one of its "words of the year." It was added to the online Oxford Dictionaries in 2014.

Consider another example. The divide between what US President Lyndon Johnson claimed about American successes or near successes or anticipated successes in the war in Vietnam and what the general public judged to be well-founded indications of failure came to be known as the "credibility gap," apparently an invention of a copy editor at the *New York Herald Tribune* for a story not about Vietnam at all but about US intervention in the Dominican Republic.[4] Or think of journalist Fareed Zakaria, who named the growth of a new form of government – the elected dictator or autocrat – "illiberal democracy" in an article in *Foreign Affairs* in 1997.[5] Columnist Joseph Kraft came up with "middle America" (in a piece published June 23, 1968 – a term Richard Nixon picked up while campaigning for President).

Evidence That Journalism Matters (or Doesn't)

Bernard Baruch, the politically influential financier, used the term "Cold War" in a speech in 1947 – a speech written by journalist Herbert Bayard Swope, and then circulated widely some months later by Walter Lippmann in his syndicated column.[6]

Can it be said that any of these terms "changed thinking" in the world?

Clearly they did just that. Words are tools that help us think, the basic software through which thinking happens. When a person's vocabulary expands, it becomes possible for that person to express more subtle and complex ideas or to share more precisely his or her perceptions of the world – indeed, to facilitate different perceptions. When a new word touches a nerve and spreads rapidly like "mansplaining" or "Cold War," it changes public thought.

"Mansplaining" is a word. It is also, we could say, a "meme" – itself quite a new word (originated by geneticist Richard Dawkins in 1976 to discuss features of human culture that replicate not through genetic transmission but through cultural transmission). Originality in journalism – at least one strong measure of it – consists in identifying new developments in society and circulating them in public and, with ingenuity and luck, inventing a term for them. Journalism is a primary site for the manufacturing of memes.

But there is no award or honor that comes with this. Dawkins won no academic or journalistic prize for "meme" nor did Solnit for "mansplaining." An academic who arrives at a new idea in relation to an existing discourse will arrive at some level of fame within a discipline or subdiscipline through the academic mode of self-replication: citations. But Fareed Zakaria collects no royalties each time someone writes "illiberal democracy" nor does any other journalist who either invented a widely used term or intervened in a novel term's circulating and recirculating. Journalists are supposed to be keenly attuned to the shifting cultural and political, social and economic tone of the times, sensitive to slight perturbations in the cultural air, and a little ahead of the rest of us in giving linguistic form to something stirring. The public world day in and day out needs registration. It needs naming for us to know it or know that we know it. This is a principal job for journalism.

Making Relevant New Information Available

Journalism offers new information that people accept as reliable and on which they base important decisions in their own lives.

The simplest example, as we noted in chapter 1, is the weather report. If journalism did not offer us weather reports, some other service might. In fact, "the weather" is the department of news most frequently consulted by audiences in both the US and the UK.[7] It is, as the saying goes, "news you can use." Health information is another much consulted category of news. Health information appears not only in columns on science or medicine but also in stories concerning, say, the health of celebrities or other prominent figures. When a celebrity has an illness, people pay heed and they may accordingly make adjustments in their own health-related habits or health-care-seeking. After US President Ronald Reagan had a widely reported cancerous tumor removed from his colon, telephone inquiries to national health information sources skyrocketed, more people went in for colon cancer screening, and almost certainly more colon cancers were detected earlier than would otherwise have been the case.[8]

The most studied arena where information in the news media is thought to influence behavior concerns whether political news in the media shapes how citizens vote. Evidence across multiple democracies indicates that the better informed people are, the more likely they are to participate in a variety of political actions, from signing petitions to discussing politics among friends to voting. But it is not clear what comes first: do the habits of participation lead to becoming more informed or does becoming better informed lead to participation?

People seek and can find information about parties and candidates during elections. A study of what political information is available on television (still the primary source of political information for most citizens in most countries) shows it to be substantial in the six nations studied: Norway, Sweden, Belgium, Netherlands, the UK, and the US. Televised political information is available and increasingly useful because growing percentages of the population do not remain loyal to a single party across elections. In the multi-party states of Norway, Sweden, Belgium, and the Netherlands, about a third of the electorate now votes for a different party from one election to the next. In the past, many more voters stayed loyal to a single party over time. Correspondingly, voters increasingly delay deciding what party to support until the election campaign (about half the population in these countries) and especially until the final few days of a campaign (about a third of these populations).[9] This means news has become a more powerful influence on voters than it used to be – not from any virtue or failing in the news media but because more people have begun making decisions about voting rather than acting habitually.

Relevant new information comprises much more than the weather report, much more than politics. It may be information about new films or TV shows, new books or a newly scheduled concert. It may be news about developments in science or medicine. It may be "social empathy" news in which reporters tell audiences about individuals or communities in their midst or half-way around the world whose lives have "human interest" appeal. They face troubles or surmount difficulties that may give readers or viewers a glimpse into how someone or some group of people with little public face or public identity make their way in the world. This can – or at least is intended to – give recognition to the normally unrecognized and instill in audiences an understanding of, and perhaps fellow feeling for, these other people.[10]

Holding Power Accountable

Journalism holds government officials and government agencies and sometimes other sources of power accountable to the public for their actions.

At the extreme, this reporting causes embarrassments that force top officials to resign or to be dismissed. US news reporting has been responsible for the removal, either by resignation or by dismissal, of multiple high-level government officials in the administration of President Donald Trump, including Cabinet officers and top national security presidential advisors. The journalist's job of "following the story" may be uncomfortable when the story unearths unpleasant truths about favored policies or persons. Professional journalists follow the story, nonetheless. Where did the news originate about Hillary Clinton's use of a private email server for official State Department business, some of it highly confidential, when she was Secretary of State? From work done by reporters for the *New York Times*. The *Times* endorsed Clinton over Trump. And I do not doubt that most reporters at that newspaper tend to have liberal sympathies. What I deny – strenuously – is that professional reporters give them free rein. It would be surprising if reporters at the *Times* were not generally liberal in their sympathies. After all, they live in New York City or in nearby suburbs. They are overwhelmingly college-educated. New York City votes Democratic even when New York State sometimes does not. If there is a bastion of cosmopolitanism in the United States, this is it. But *New York Times* journalists take pride in their allegiance to professional values of accuracy, truth-seeking, fairness, objectivity, and following the story – wherever it leads.

Sometimes, of course, governments are forced to respond to interventions in shaping the public agenda by agents other than political journalists. Social movements, for instance, challenge widespread assumptions, change public language, and force political change – whether Gandhi's *satyagraha* in India almost a century ago, the civil rights movement in the US several generations ago, the *gilets jaunes* in France today, or the #MeToo movement that brought the US in 2017 (and very quickly thereafter many other countries around the world) a new language for and a new fervor about sexual harassment and sexual abuse in the workplace and beyond. Activist women initiated #MeToo but journalism still played a key role in its spread nationally and globally through extensive investigative reports in the *New Yorker* and the *New York Times* concerning allegations of sexual abuse against Hollywood producer Harvey Weinstein.

So social movements may effectively challenge the powerful in government, in corporations, and in other institutions. So may minority political parties. So may relentless individuals in pursuit of a cause. But in terms of day-to-day monitoring of government power, nothing is more important than the news media – both for directly challenging government authority and for reporting on the organizations, movements, and individuals who do their own challenging.

Journalism, by virtue of its habits of cooking reality into a digestible casserole, has become a screening committee for political candidates seeking office, for new medications or new technological innovations seeking a market, for new books or music or up-and-coming athletes or actors or apps. Journalists do not operate independently of other social forces, of course. Pharmaceutical companies, medical researchers, and government health regulators have enormous, often decisive, influence on what medications reach the public. Organized political parties have continuing power over candidate grooming and candidate selection, but that power has weakened as party-directed candidate selection shifts toward "audience democracy."[11] This is especially true in the United States, where a system of primary elections may bring a dozen or two dozen potential candidates into the ring, all vying for public attention and approval to win a party's nomination, but features of "audience democracy" can now be found in democracies around the world.

There is no settled answer to the question of how

influential journalism is nor even a simple listing of the conditions under which the news media may matter more or less. If there were, businesses would know – and not guess – how to spend their advertising dollars and politicians would be able to run for office only when they were certain or nearly certain they would win. It doesn't work that way.

6

Why Technology is Not the Whole Story

Does the Internet change everything? Yes and no.

Obviously – perhaps too obviously – technology matters. It is pretty easy to recognize that if you want to write on paper, a pencil will be far more useful than a hammer, and if you want to secure two pieces of wood together with a nail, a hammer will work better than a pencil. Is it possible to write with a hammer (in mud or clay or wet cement) or pound with a pencil? Yes, but it will be slow and awkward. There is something about a technology that directs us to make use of it in some ways and not others, and that empowers us to achieve certain ends that otherwise would be much more difficult to accomplish.

These features of technologies are sometimes seen as intended or unintended "biases." If you call my relatively modest height an anti-basketball bias, that would not be wrong, but more likely you would call it a feature or facet of Michael Schudson that makes it unlikely that he could have had a career as a professional basketball player. The features of a technology that direct us – not force us – down a certain path are what scholars of technology often call "affordances": the opportunities for action that a particular thing or particular environment provides. The concept came from studies of ecology in which different natural features – a rock or a river, say – "afforded" different uses for different species (for some species a rock is a shelter and for others it is a place to sun oneself; for some species a river is the environment for food and for others it serves as a place to drink). This applies to technology, too. A pencil may be, and usually is, in relation to an adult human, a tool for writing; the same pencil may be, and often is, in relation to a child, a weapon for attacking or annoying siblings.

Unlike features of nature, human-made technologies have certain purposes built into them. They have been engineered toward specific ends. What we experience as technology is not necessarily fixed in the thing-itself but the thing-as-conceived and therefore the thing-as-constructed by our fellow humans. And, yes, one might sometimes recognize some of this purpose-driven-ness of technology to be a "bias." The operation of the standard scissors favors right-handed people; it can be used by lefties with the left hand but it is more difficult. Hand-written communications in left-to-right scripts are likewise biased against lefties. The words you have written on a line remain visible to the righty. They are covered up by your left hand if you write as a lefty.

Some technologies are relatively standard and unchanging. Some are not. For a standard technology, consider the spoon: you may use a spoon to shovel food into your mouth or you may use it to measure your coffee, but its solidity and its simplicity seem to make it relatively immune to alterations. Other technologies are far more open to interpretation and negotiation. The difference between relatively flexible and relatively inflexible technologies is approximated by the now familiar terms "hardware" and "software." The latter often operate within a framework that the former supplies. The software is much more variable, much more subject to human interventions, even by relatively inexpert humans.[1]

We can see this in the history of a relatively old technology: the book. Books as we have known them even hundreds of years before Gutenberg are in "codex" form. The codex, as opposed to the scroll, has among its affordances random (rather than sequential) access for the user so that a reader can dip into the book at any point, unlike the scroll, where the reader has to laboriously unroll all of the scroll until reaching the passage sought. This is a great advantage and the codex began to replace the scroll almost as soon as it was invented. In Egypt by the fifth century, the codex outnumbered the scroll by ten to one based on surviving examples, and by the sixth century the scroll had almost vanished from use.

Once the basic codex form of the book was settled and later became more easily reproducible with the printing press, the evolution of the "book" had its software updated in ways that made it increasingly useful to readers. People complained 400 years ago that there was a problem of "too much information."[2] A variety of software "fixes" for this problem emerged. Printers began to provide page numbers and punctuation. They broke books up into chapters and introduced chapter titles. They used "running heads" at the top of the page. They introduced the table of contents. The codex hardware made "random access" possible but it took this new "software," if you will, to make access practical, convenient, and actually useable.

The concept of affordance locates middle ground

between a position that technologies are simply elements in human activity that, like all other elements, we can adapt just as we choose and a stance that technologies are powerful and inflexible forces that determine our behavior. Neither extreme seems to offer a very useful general theory. The notion of an all-powerful technology that dictates its uses is inconsistent with the succession of social and technical innovations that have led a particular technology – say, the printing press – to take on quite different roles in different times and places. The printing press at first was used to print the Bible and volumes of sermons more than scientific treatises or political pamphlets; it did more during its first century to reinforce social and political hierarchies than to catalyze social change. Even when a technology's employment seems to arrive at a fairly standard repertoire of uses, other forces – rather than the technological affordances as such – shape which of these will be adopted. Thus public service broadcasting has been enormously influential in most of Western Europe for nearly the full history of radio and television broadcasting, but not in the United States. Same technology, but sharply different political, cultural, economic, and social environments.

Taking technology to invariably be the prime

mover of changes in human communication is a lazy substitute for thinking through what kinds of innovations have really mattered in the history of communications – and how. Historian Wolfgang Behringer engagingly makes the case that the biggest change in European communications can be traced not to the printing press, turnpike, railroad, telegraph, submarine cable, telephone, and so forth, up to the Internet, but to the emergence of a European postal system. The decisive innovation was "an organizational invention, not a technological one."[3] The great innovation was to improve the speed of transmitting the mail by locating multiple stations for changing horses and riders along the mail routes. The stations were called "posts" and the system was first developed and staffed by Italians who also gave it its name – "*posta*."

People are so mesmerized today by digital technology that we – this includes journalists themselves – fail to recognize non-technological sources of change; we also downplay the ingenuity and the consequences of software innovation as well as hardware. One of the most important transformations of journalism in the past century was not the rise of television news in the 1950s and 1960s but the rise of a more investigative, more analytical, and more critical journalism (largely in print rather than in radio or television) in the 1960s and 1970s in Europe, North America, and soon thereafter Latin America and elsewhere. The very phrases "watchdog" press or "accountability reporting" are rarely used before this era. The amount and percentage of this deeper and more assertive journalism in newspapers grew by leaps and bounds after the 1960s in the US, displacing strictly "objective" reporting in essentially all leading news organizations.

Why? There are various explanations, but none that rest on technology as a significant factor or any factor at all. The rise of democracy was one force itself toward legitimating the views of ordinary people and encouraging them to question their rulers; the rise of organized science was over time successful in establishing a new form of authority not closely linked to governmental power; shifts in higher education since World War II led college and university instruction to emphasize critical thinking more than the transmission of a specific cultural heritage or authoritative canon. All this and more contributed to the growth of more analytical journalism – but a direct role for technology as such? No.

So much for a general framework about the role of technology in society. Now to the impact specifically of digital technologies, the Internet, and social media on journalism. The argument is strong that we are in the endgame of the distribution of news on paper.[4] This is most true in the United States, less so in countries where the news business was never so dependent on advertising revenue for its survival. Even so, the seismic tremors of change are felt in most parts of the world.

But where does this change come from and where is it going? Before Facebook and Google, there was already economic distress in the news business. Newspapers were losing readers to television news, one sign of which is that not only were daily newspapers dying but their decline in the US was much sharper for those that published in the afternoon – more directly in competition with the evening national and local TV news broadcasts – than those published in the morning. The decline of standard print journalism in economic viability was accompanied by a drop in general public credibility. A 2012 study of the newspaper press in the US, the UK, Finland, Germany, France, and Italy found that in all six countries more than 60 percent of adults claimed "not very much" or "no" confidence in the press and "in every one of the countries covered, this symbolic crisis predates the rise of digital media."[5]

A statement of the gravity of the situation was expressed in 2014 by the late David Carr, the savvy media reporter for the *New York Times*, who noted that three major US news companies – Gannett, Tribune Company, and E. W. Scripps – had just spun off their newspaper properties from their multi-media empires. The flurry of divestitures, he wrote, looked like "one of those movies about global warming where icebergs calve huge chunks into churning waters." Carr's metaphors grew even more alarming. He compared divesting the newspaper properties after a decade of stripping them of their resources to "trashing a house by burning all the furniture to stay warm and then inviting people in to see if they want to buy the joint." And while he blamed "the natural order" of the marketplace, he found no solace or hope in the public. Many people, he wrote, "haven't cared or noticed as their hometown newspapers have reduced staffing, days of circulation, delivery and coverage." Are they likely to notice or care "when those newspapers go away altogether? I'm not optimistic about that."[6]

This is the same man who had stood up at the podium of a 2009 journalism conference to make some remarks, then returned to the speakers' table to pick up his laptop and, holding it up above his head as he returned to the podium, declared, "I have more resources for reporting in my hand at this moment than in any newsroom I have ever worked in."[7] It was a simple, dramatic gesture and there was no doubt that he was right. He was right for reporters and editors. He was right, too, for news consumers, who also have laptops and can access the websites of hundreds, thousands of news organizations and government agencies and think tanks and much more, around the world. It is a brave new world for information. (Of course, had he spoken to a conference in 2014 and not 2009, he would not have had to go back to the speakers' table for his laptop but would have reached into his pocket for his phone.)

Should we embrace Carr's awestruck wonder of 2009? Or his despair of 2014?

Let's be clear: there are scarcely any national "newspapers" any more as stand-alone enterprises; most of them around the world are merged print-and-online businesses. Local news organizations are moving in the same direction. Many of the most popular websites for news are the websites of what used to be print or broadcast news organizations – in the US the top three news websites are digital natives but the next 12 of the top 15 are legacy news organization websites.[8] Those organizations are changing, and scrambling, and thinning, but not generally speaking disappearing. In a few instances, they are growing in reach, in status, and in global influence – in the UK the *Guardian* and the *Financial Times*, and in the US the *New York Times*, come quickly to mind.

The newsrooms' population of journalists has been shrinking more rapidly than the quantity of serious journalism they produce. How sure can we be that, in fact, serious journalism is shrinking at all?

If what really matters for social and civic welfare is not the disappearance of a paper product tossed on the doorstep or purchased at a news stand but the thinning of fair-minded, analytical, and watch-dog news reporting, how much of a decline – if any – are we witnessing? If such news can be provided by some means other than newspapers and by some organizations or mechanisms able to pay for a bureau in Beijing or Baghdad, the civic value of journalism can be sustained.

There are more than 1,200 daily printed news-papers in the United States, even though essentially all of them are part of businesses that also publish online. Few of them have ever won a Pulitzer Prize or opened a foreign bureau or supported a full-time foreign correspondent. It could, of course, be worse – and it was. Carl Sessions Stepp compared major daily newspapers in 1964 and 1999 and concluded – I cannot imagine any other conclusion possible

– that the 1999 papers were "by almost any measure, far superior to their 1960s counterparts: better written, better looking, better organized, more responsible, less sensational, less sexist and racist, and more informative and public-spirited than they are often given credit for."[9]

Stepp's study is an informed judgment about the US case. Dutch media historian Marcel Broersma makes a comparable judgment about the European press. Thinking of Dutch media specifically and European and North Atlantic media more broadly, Broersma has written:

> Open a random newspaper of 20 years ago or watch an old television newscast and you will see a different journalism, but one that is overall not as good as it is now. Journalism is more complete, diverse, analytical and critical. It is quicker, less institutional and more relevant to audiences. . . . Whichever way you look at it, the news consumer is certainly better served.[10]

In the US, a recent examination of a dozen large and medium-sized regional daily newspapers found not a decrease but a notable increase in investigative reporting. Former CBS News correspondent Beth Knobel analyzed the content of these newspapers for selected years between 1991 and 2011 and, to her surprise, found a notable increase in original, accountability-oriented enterprise reporting – despite the fact that the newspapers she examined, like so many others, had laid off many journalists in the same years. Based on interviews she conducted with editors at these newspapers, she cites three reasons. First and foremost, the journalists at these papers believed that "accountability reporting" was their core mission. Second, since US television, throughout its history, has done very little enterprise reporting, newspapers made an economic choice to drop some lighter fare in their news operation and stick with the distinctive kind of hard-hitting investigations that broadcast rivals were not doing. They felt that, in the long run, this was an investment in economic survival. And, third, the cost of doing accountability reporting had declined thanks to the very Internet that was proving to be the newspapers' economic nemesis . "The advent of the Internet made it easier to find people and contact them via e-mail, access government databases, file Freedom of Information Act requests, and use complex computer-assisted reporting technologies."[11] In the US case, the greatest worry about declining journalism is that many communities are losing their only substantial local news outlets. What have come to be called "news deserts" are turning up in small towns across the country as economically failing newspapers close down. For a country where in the nineteenth century the establishment of a local newspaper was a key indicator that a town had aspirations for economic growth and development, this is a very troubling trend.

7

Journalism's Four Non-Revolutions

The technological transformation of journalism in the past two decades has understandably led to multiple claims about both the glorious flowering of a new journalism and the utter destruction of everything worthwhile in the old journalism. Neither utopian nor dystopian assessments look safe. And while many of the new developments have been very important, their birth and influence have not necessarily spelled the demise of earlier journalistic institutions, genres, or habits of work. Radio did not destroy newspapers but lived off of the news-gathering the newspapers continued to do. Television did not kill newspapers either. I do not think digital media will make newspapers obsolete soon or, indeed, ever. But the news organizations that have long produced newspapers are now essentially all producing news online and some have either abandoned paper altogether or have restricted the paper edition's distribution.

People respond to changes around them with the hopes and fears they bring with them to any social change, but especially to changes whose technological embodiment immediately advertises itself (literally and figuratively) as revolutionary. It is no wonder that digital media have inspired utopian and dystopian visions.

Of course, the technology-launched changes have been real and profound – and fast. Older journalists have watched a collapse of what they took to be either eternal journalism or triumphant journalism that had successfully supplanted a somewhat sordid but more distant past. Jack Fuller, who ultimately served as editor of the *Chicago Tribune*, recalls beginning at that paper in the early 1960s when "reporters typed their stories on manual typewriters." "Copyboys"—as both young men and women were called – took those stories from one desk to the next to the linotype machine operators in the composing room. The *Tribune* was in this respect like every other newspaper of the day.[1]

Nearly a decade later and an ocean away, Alan Rusbridger, editor-in-chief of the *Guardian* from 1995 to 2015, similarly marveled at the rapid changes he had personally witnessed. In 1995, he writes, "we printed stories on newsprint, produced once a day. By the time I stepped down 20 years later, that world had been turned upside down. By then, just 6 per cent of young (18- to 24-year-old) readers were getting their news from print; 65 per cent were relying on online sources, including social media, for their news." He is awed by the speed and power of the changes. They are a "Force-12 hurricane of disruption"; "The vertical world is gone for ever"; there is a "total inversion of how news is created, shared, and distributed"; it is a "sea change in mass communications."[2]

Only it is not, in fact, a "total inversion." There are two central, overarching features of contemporary change that Rusbridger overlooks. First, news dissemination has changed far more than news-gathering. Those news organizations – it would be anachronistic to call them newspapers – that still produce among their products print-on-dead-trees remain the primary news-gatherers of the world, along with the so-called "wire services" (notably Associated Press, Reuters, Agence France Presse). These organizations produce the preponderance of original news – reported, compelling, and assertive – that television journalism lives off of and that online social media recirculate. The primary engine of news-gathering remains largely the same news organizations that have been the leading lights of journalism for generations.

Second, with all of the changes in politics and journalism of the past two decades, the same old news organizations that publish newspapers (in print and digitally), along with, in Europe, leading public broadcasting systems, set the public agenda just as much today as they did 25 years ago. That conclusion is supported by a careful study of Swedish media coverage in relation to what issues the general public thinks are most important. It is not that Swedish newspapers and public broadcasters have not seen sharp declines in the size of their audiences, and it is not that the Swedish newspaper organizations have not seen landslide losses in advertising revenue; even so, in public consciousness, directly or indirectly, these "gatekeepers" lead in setting the public agenda as they have in the past.[3]

The world of journalism is in the midst of great changes, but it may be not quite the "revolution" it seems to be. Consider the following four candidates for characterizing a media revolution.

Journalism's Four Non-Revolutions

From Professional Journalism to Citizen Journalism

No one can doubt that "citizens" who have never thought of themselves as journalists, never aspired to be journalists, and never for a second speculated about what journalism is or should be, have increasingly functioned as journalists. That is, they have come upon "news" events, they have "gathered" that news by photographically recording it on their cell phones or by narrating it on their phones as they watched and recorded it, and they have provided that news instantaneously to Facebook friends or directly to news organizations. If they have not done so spontaneously and independently, they have sometimes responded to calls from news organizations to "crowd-source" a topic, sending in to a professional news organization their reports of how some phenomenon is manifesting itself in their town or neighborhood.

Yes, crowd-sourcing has happened before, at least as far back as the 1700s in British North America. And for much of the history of journalism – most of which happened before professional journalism arose – the content of newspapers was provided to a printer by voluntary and unpaid contributions from ordinary citizens. In the history of journalism, citizen journalism preceded professional journalism. It has never fully disappeared. But in the age of professional journalism, new technologies – most of all the mobile phone with Internet connectivity and photographic capability – have revived citizen journalism and made it more important today than it has been in the past 100 years.

That said, citizen journalism provides a very small amount of the original reported content of what appears in the products, both online and on paper, of leading news organizations, be they hybrid online/print newspapers or broadcast or cable television, or the most widely read news sites online. What percentage of news on all of these outlets comes from citizen journalists? I don't know. My guess would be less than 5 percent. That said, citizen journalism demonstrates value in situations where a free press does not exist, where "news deserts" emerge, and where military conflict or political anarchy makes the visibility of professional journalists exceedingly dangerous – as in, for instance, today's Syrian civil war.

From Print Journalism to Digital Journalism

This is a kind of revolution indeed, with much revolutionary potential still ahead, but in two respects it has been exaggerated. First, the shift is not from print to digital but from print to print-and-digital. As a business proposition, the paper edition remains valuable to many news organizations; the people who want their paper edition pay premium prices for it and they help to underwrite the online operation. And even when important breaking news runs first on the website, the "front page" of the print edition has retained symbolic significance – both for journalists themselves and for the general public. When media scholar Nikki Usher spent five months in 2010 inside the *New York Times* newsroom, she found journalists "stuck in a print-first mentality." She wrote that "print still retains its aura of mystique and importance."[4] That is less true a decade later, but, even so, the news organization's website is for now while the front page is for "tomorrow" and beyond. That is, the front page, frozen at one moment, is more available as a historical record than the ever-changing news on the webpage.

Second, in the US and UK as in many other parts of the world, most people get their news from television. People may increasingly access that news on their mobile phones, but what they access is television-produced news. In 2013, 69 percent of people listed television as one of their two "main" source of news, 50 percent digital sources, and 28 percent newspapers.[5] Television is easy and convenient, and that is not a bad thing. It communicates the basics, sometimes vividly, which is about as much as most of us can absorb most of the time. For about 50 years, more Americans have reported television as their primary source of news rather than newspapers. Most people do not know or do not care that television gets *its* news from newspaper organizations.

Television's reach notwithstanding, there remains a market for "long-form" printed journalism, very long form. Consider the fact that at least 15 books have been produced by American journalists about the wars in Iraq and Afghanistan. These were the work of correspondents who have covered those wars for NBC, National Public Radio, the magazines *US News*, *Newsweek*, and the *New Yorker*, as well as two different *Wall Street Journal* reporters, a *New York Times* military reporter, a *Chicago Tribune* reporter, and at least half a dozen *Washington Post* reporters. Cute cat videos and angry tweets have not replaced long-form journalism. There is more book-length journalism than ever.

From Stories to Databases

When it comes to journalism emerging from and contributing to large databases suitable for analysis and potentially generative of news stories, the possibilities are considerable. The Panama Papers (2016), for instance, was a massive leak of 11.5 million documents. The Paradise Papers (2017) a year later, was a leak of 14.3 million documents.[6]

The databases matter. The capacity to store such large amounts of data and to process it has no precedent in the history of journalism. New courses of study on computational journalism or data journalism have arisen at journalism schools around the world. Still, even as databases become public, few people access them directly. Most readers want someone – let us call that someone a "journalist" – to turn a database into a story. That person should have a sense and a sensibility about what a story is and how to tame a seemingly endless parade of facts and figures into a narrative that can be told in relatively conventional ways that relatively untutored readers can grasp. What readers may have an appetite for and a cognitive grasp of is a story, and the journalist is under greater pressure than ever to squeeze from these databases something that can fit into story form.

It is worth adding that the economic crisis in journalism has a direct influence on the geography of data journalism. Small news organizations cannot hire a data journalism specialists, or keep them if they do. They gravitate quickly to large news organizations.[7]

From Top-Down (Vertical) to Shareable (Horizontal) Communication

"Sharing" is one of the key words of our time.[8] It is not just a description of the ease and frequency with which people transmit words, news stories, photographs, quips, and quotes, recirculating materials of humor or of outrage that they have received online from others in their online worlds. It is also an ethic, and one that implies that one shares something of one's "self." The very idea of sharing implies something warm-hearted, expressive, personal, and even confessional.

There is in news production a growing emphasis on making news stories shareable and encouraging that they be shared. News organizations urge their reporters not only to write stories but also to market them on social media, and there is something of a shift from the professional focus on "newsworthiness" in a story to a more business-centered emphasis on what a Dutch study has dubbed "shareworthiness."[9]

That said, we have scarcely abandoned top-down

communication. And we are far from seeing the end of professional journalism in its "gatekeeping" role in public life. Professional journalists still have a place in a world where so much communication is online and so much of it is on social media, where it is hard for people to keep in mind where their information comes from. Half of the people on Facebook report that they do not understand why some items are posted on their Facebook news feed and not others and they have not made use of available Facebook tools to control their own news feed.[10] In this world, professional journalists continue to have a key role in deciding what enters into public discussion.

There is an uncountable amount of talk online, from email to Facebook to Twitter to comments readers post to websites, reviews they post on TripAdvisor, and active strings of comments about pregnancy and infancy posted on "What to Expect When You're Expecting." On the whole, this explosion of communications offers astonishing benefits in terms of the circulation of medical information, advice to the lovelorn, information about a place you may want to visit, information about how to reach people who share the same rare disease you have, and so on. But in this informational downpour, how much is produced by non-professional journalists that leads powerful individuals and institutions to wince, change course, retreat, or resign? In the first two years of the Trump administration, *Washington Post* reporting helped end the brief career of Michael Flynn as White House national security advisor; the *New Yorker* provided facts that destroyed the brief career of Anthony Scaramucci as White House communications director; and *Politico*, a largely online political reporting news organization begun in 2007 by two veteran *Washington Post* reporters, brought down health and human services secretary Tom Price for the petty corruption of illegitimate personal expenditures of the taxpayers' dollars. In each case, professional journalists, at old-line or at online news organizations, secured facts that had consequences. What united *Politico* with the *Washington Post* and the *New Yorker* was a commitment to fact-based, reported, story-oriented, accountability-directed journalism.

Journalists are certainly not the only "top-down" communicators. Populist political leaders, even populist heads of state, whether in the United States or in Latin America, have taken to Twitter with enthusiasm – not because Twitter enables sharing (two-way communication and multi-way communication), but because it enables them to quickly and efficiently provide one-way communication to their "followers." Sharing has grown. Two-way communication has grown and multi-directional communication has grown. One-way communication nonetheless remains in most contexts as important as ever. New digital forms of communication disrupt older forms, but they are themselves also hijacked by traditional hierarchical habits. Populist presidents in Latin America have used Twitter for one-way, top-down communication exclusively, and were doing so for at least several years before Donald Trump came to office. Trump has followed a well-worn path.[11]

We should beware a kind of romance of the horizontal, but it seems everywhere around us. It has been all over the promotional efforts of social media companies. It has been embedded deeply in utopian hopes for a digital transformation of society. It has influenced scholarship in communication for generations. US media scholar John Durham Peters has urged that Jesus giving sermons is as admirable a model of communication ("dissemination") as Socrates engaging in another fine model, "dialogue." Peters makes the point that dialogue can be despotic (it wasn't easy to argue with Socrates!) while the sermon, although top-down, gives listeners the freedom to take it or leave it.

You can walk away from a sermon, or daydream during it. Walking away from a conversation, even an abusive one, is much more difficult. Participants control each other, but the power of one is by no means equal to the power of the other, even if the two people in dialogue are nominally equals. Peters concludes that "dialogue can be tyrannical and dissemination can be just" and that dialogue is "only one communicative script among many," and one, in fact, particularly ill suited as a general model for large-scale democracy.[12]

That said, has there been a move in the era of the Internet and social media toward horizontal communications? Yes. Is it all to the good? Obviously not. Has it left vertical communication behind? Again, obviously not.

8

Is There a Future for Journalism?

Does journalism have a future? Certainly it does, although it may be wiser to say that journalism has multiple futures that will develop simultaneously. True, for more than a decade, people in and around journalism have been looking for a workable business model for professional news-gathering and, while they have found some useful pieces of an answer, nothing has emerged that looks anything like a panacea for the economic crisis that journalism faces around the world. Meanwhile, one news organization after another cuts staff jobs to save money in the face of continuing economic distress.

But a variety of enormously valuable enterprises do not have a business model. Western classical music? It survives, but without a business model. In much of Europe, it receives substantial state subsidy. In the United States, it receives very little governmental support, but it carries on nonetheless, as do many other arts, thanks to wealthy lovers of culture who are cultivated by development directors at schools, museums, symphony orchestras, opera companies, dance companies – most of which would fold quickly if they had to depend on ticket sales alone.

For a very long time, people who love the arts enough to pursue them professionally have often made ends meet with day jobs they may or may not enjoy. US poet William Carlos Williams was a physician; US-born British poet T. S. Eliot worked for Lloyd's Bank and later for Faber & Faber publishers; US composer Charles Ives had a successful career in the insurance business. A great many professional musicians teach music. Or they may work as wandering minstrels in restaurants, taking requests (and tips) from diners. My brother did that to make some money for the work he loved of composing (popular) music, although he wanted to scream each time a customer requested that he play "Moon River" yet again. When I attended a lecture-demonstration of classical music at a school of music a few years ago, the dean of the school offered some remarks after the program. He said that the school sought not only to train able musicians but also to instill an entrepreneurial spirit and entrepreneurial skills – salesmanship as well as musicianship. And I have thought about this often in imagining a future for journalism. As one of my Journalism School colleagues told me, "It's not that there are no jobs – there are no careers." There are jobs and, indeed, the move to digital journalism has meant that it has grown easier for young men or women to invent jobs for themselves.

Some aspects of journalism's future look very grim, not only for economic but also for political reasons. In certain parts of the world, even in nominally democratic countries, journalism has become an endangered species, with, for example, the government of Prime Minister Viktor Orbán in Hungary making making newspaper and television criticism of his regime essentially extinct – although online criticism still has a place. In other parts of the world, the problem is not so much repression or censorship as direct violence against journalists. Reporters have been assaulted, kidnapped, and murdered. In 2018, 54 journalists were killed for reasons related to their work as journalists, most of them specifically targeted, others caught in cross-fire in war zones. Twelve were killed in Afghanistan, ten in Syria, four in Mexico, and four in the US. (The latter four, all reporters and editors, plus a fifth person, a sales assistant, were murdered in a single mass shooting at *The Capital*, a daily newspaper in Annapolis, Maryland.)

Scarcely a day goes by when there is not word that a news organization has collapsed economically or another one has been shut down or its reporters have been imprisoned. Journalists have organized internationally to keep track of and publicize endangered journalists, notably through the Committee to Protect Journalists (founded in 1981). In a recent report CPJ calls the jailing of journalists "the new normal," with 250 or more reporters imprisoned in 2016, 2017, and 2018.[1] Turkey, China, and Egypt have led the list in each year, accounting for half of the world's jailed journalists.

It is worth mentioning a new organization aptly called the Center for Media at Risk, established in 2018 by Barbie Zelizer, the Raymond Williams Professor of Communication at the Annenberg School for Communication, University of Pennsylvania. The Center seeks to increase public awareness concerning safety for journalists, photojournalists, videographers, filmmakers, and others, and to increase and improve the critical study of threats to a free media environment.

Even for others who only report about violence rather than having been subjected to it, there's enough tension, anxiety, and, in the end, trauma to the work of journalism that reporters seek counseling to handle the pressures and perils. Reporters may be subjected to anger or threats from their sources or their subjects. They may be harassed by criticism on social media or trolling. The Dart Center on Trauma and Journalism provides guidance and referrals for journalists in that situation. Bruce Shapiro, executive director of the Dart Center, notes that studies over the past 20 years show that, overall, journalists are quite resilient in the face of these concerns. Some 6 to 13 percent have suffered from PTSD – roughly the same percentage as in other "first responder" fields like fire fighters or police officers.[2]

In some respects, journalism's future looks remarkably bright. Think about the International Consortium of Investigative Journalists (ICIJ). Founded by the Center for Public Integrity (Washington, DC) in 1997, it became an independent organization in 2017. Even by 2000, it included 75 journalists in 39 countries; today it includes some 200 journalists at 100 different media organizations in 70 countries. In 2017, ICIJ received a Pulitzer Prize for "explanatory reporting" for its work on the Panama Papers investigation.

While ICIJ is an unusual organization in its size and the extent of its success, it is not unusual for new journalism ventures in the digital era – on two counts. First, it is cooperative and collaborative across news organizations; and, second, its collaborations are global. This is now true of many new news initiatives when, a generation ago, it was rare. In fact, in those ancient days of 1990 or 2000, collaboration with other news organizations was taken to be a kind of treason to the underlying competitiveness of journalism as a business.

Another novel development are fact-checking organizations. Independent fact-checking organizations – those not developed within and for existing news organizations – began first in the United States, with FactCheck.org in 2003 and PolitiFact in 2007. With remarkable speed, the idea traveled around the world. In Britain, Channel 4 Fact Check began in 2005, a French fact-check, Désintox, emerged in 2008, a Serbian effort, Istinomer, in 2009, 20 others in seven countries in 2010, and at last count (thanks to Duke Reporters' Lab in 2019) there are close to 200 fact-checking outlets in more than 60 countries. FactCheck.org and PolitiFact have counseled fact-checking organizations in South America, Africa, Australia, and Europe. Not all of the fact-checking efforts operate quite the same way, but all of them accept and proudly claim kinship with the others as part of a movement in journalism.[3]

Other news initiatives also have demonstrated success. Novelty seems to be everywhere online. Blogs have become indispensable "go-to" sites in a wide variety of specialized fields of inquiry. In the *Wall Street Journal*'s investigation of the highly touted Silicon Valley start-up that promoted its medical testing devices, a turning point for *Journal* reporter John Carreyrou was a tip pointing to likely fraudulence at the company. It came from Adam Clapper, a private individual who ran "Pathology Blawg." Carreyrou knew the blog, had reason to trust it, and this was a first step to his sensational revelations and a dramatic account of them in his book *Bad Blood*.[4] And then there are all the online communications auxiliary to basic news reporting that bring reporter and reader closer together in the ease and convenience of reader feedback (which is not to ignore the downside to such feedback in rude, vulgar, and even threatening comments).

My forecast for journalism is neither for a bright, sunny day nor for a torrential downpour. I see gray skies with periods of sunshine or sunshine with periods of gray. The best to hope for is that people who care about the good that journalism can do will be steadfast and resolute. Journalism cannot do what political institutions fail to do. It cannot do its work when state censorship or intimidation prevents it. It cannot operate well without the public's good will. It cannot thrive if private organizations in "civil society" do not supplement its efforts with their own, doing their own fact-finding and also endorsing or leading legal efforts to protect free speech and a free press.

It may not come as a surprise that some people suggested to me that it would be irresponsible to write a book that holds that journalism has a future. After all, I might encourage some starry-eyed young people to aim for a career in journalism when no such career will exist in five or ten or twenty years. But I find that an unrealistic stance. The fault in it is not that the economic prospects for journalism are glorious – they are not – but that the joy of working in the field has been and remains great for some and utterly irresistible for others.

There are multiple dimensions of that joy. One is that in journalism a person can make a big difference to the public good – and can do so at quite a young age. As one Afghan journalist said, "It's not like the past where you had to wait until you were 40 or 45 years old to make an impact on Afghan society. This new media provides an opportunity for the new generation."[5]

Journalism provides other opportunities. The opportunity to be in the know. The chance to feel that every word matters. Alan Rusbridger reports his conversation with Marty Baron, executive editor of the *Washington Post*, who said he always looks to hire optimists – and Rusbridger agreed.[6] They are looking not for idiots or for saints ready to sacrifice themselves for a cause but for people who believe in a future that they could, with effort, move toward, in organizations that also believe in a future.

"I don't follow the news," one teenager told media scholars Lynn Schofield and Regina Marchi a few years ago. "But, Twitter is almost like the news. I have it on my phone and if I'm holding my phone it's like an instinct. I just go to it. If something's going on, everyone's talking about it on Twitter."[7] Twitter, indeed, is "almost" like the news, a widely accessed omnibus of professional news and personal gossip, comment, aggregation, and relay. Here, as on Facebook and other social media, the "public sphere" has been refashioned as a public/private sphere – as it had been in the coffee houses and pubs that German philosopher Jürgen Habermas discussed as the original location of a non-sponsored (not government-controlled and not church-managed) arena for people to come together to freely – and more or less equally – discuss public events and issues, often doing so in relation to some provocation in a newspaper.[8]

Is There a Future for Journalism?

To see Twitter as a medium that helps constitute a "public" (or "public/private") sphere may raise the dignity of Twitter or it may lower the dignity of the so-called "public sphere" of eighteenth-century Western Europe. Habermas was doing his best in his 1962 study of the emergence of a "public sphere" to imagine what conversation might have been like in eighteenth-century taverns and coffee houses where, in his view, a public life free from state or church repression, first appeared. But several decades later historian Robert Darnton did not have to imagine the talk in those public spaces; he found detailed reports of it filed by the king's secret police after they eavesdropped in the bars and coffee houses of Paris. These conversations, if we can believe the police reports (and we should take them with a grain of salt), make it clear that people who talked in public settings were willing to criticize the king.

But why was the king under scrutiny? For his sex life. For his mistresses who seemed able to manipulate him as they wished. For his philandering in ways that reduced the dignity of his office.[9]

More than 250 years later, governments still eavesdrop on private citizens, although this is judged to be scandalous when we learn about it. More than 250 years later, the effort to construct a public sphere, even in the liberal democracies that take such aspiration seriously, remains woefully incomplete. Meanwhile, those who proclaim that we live in a "post-truth" era all but abandon the effort. Many academics, like many journalists, like many others, grab at various clichés and memes and clever phrases as handholds in a complex and baffling world. But the "post-truth" cliché cannot be accepted by anyone serious about where we are and where we should be going. We do not live in and we could not live in a "post-truth" world.

John F. Kennedy was assassinated in Dallas, Texas, in 1963. The Berlin Wall came down in 1989 – not exactly in the way it has mythically been remembered, but the divide between East Germany and West Germany was decisively breached and the world has in fact been a different place ever since.[10] There are millions of facts we believe in even when we do not have personal knowledge of them. And, most of the time, we are correct in doing so. That's how the world – usually – works. That's how people manage to get across the street safely. That's how people get from dawn to dusk.

The most decisive case against any society ever being a "post-truth" society was put simply by Walter Lippmann a century ago. While he made a general argument that "the way in which the world is imagined determines at any particular moment

114

what men will do," he immediately added, "It does not determine what they will achieve. It determines their effort, their feelings, their hopes, not their accomplishments and results."[11] You may purchase the Brooklyn Bridge from a street vendor but, sorry, you will not thereby own it. You may think you can attain immortal life by buying a potion from a traveling salesperson – that, after all, is what the salesperson promises. You have helped sustain one liar's livelihood, but you will die in due course nonetheless.

Can we be mistaken about facts? Of course. Can even conscientious journalists get the story wrong? Of course. Can even scientists be wrong? Certainly. Science is a human institution and all of our products are fallible. What gives science its authority is that it subjects its conclusions to rigorous critique again and again in a community of critical thinkers dedicated to knowing the world better.

Fallibility is our middle name. But the conscientious effort to ascertain the facts and to get the story right and to stand tall rather than bow to hucksters on our doorsteps or high officials who seek our dollars or our votes or simply our submission – those conscientious efforts make a difference. In the world of journalism, conscientious effort has grown more substantial and sophisticated around the world, and in liberal societies, under threat though they are, journalism has increasingly achieved the power to withstand both market forces and malignant politicians. Journalism matters in this complicated world – and as it is something that matters you can sign your name to it and make a difference.

Notes

Chapter 1 Introduction

1 John Hersey, "The Legend on the License," *Yale Review* 70 (1980), 1–25 at 2 (1980).
2 Thomas S. Crane, Letter to the Editor, *New York Times*, May 9, 2019.
3 Cited in Marion Marzolf, "American 'New Journalism' Takes Root in Europe at End of 19th Century," *Journalism Quarterly* 61 (1984), 529–36, 691 at 531.
4 Alan Rusbridger, *Breaking News: The Remaking of Journalism and Why It Matters Now* (New York: Farrar Straus Giroux, 2018), p. 335.

Chapter 2 What Kind of Journalism Matters Most?

1 Rusbridger, *Breaking News*, p. 7.
2 Henrik Ornebring, "Journalism as Institution and Work in Europe, Circa 1860: A Comparative History of Journalism," *Media History* 19, no. 4 (2013), 393–407.

3 Donald Matheson, "The Birth of News Discourse: Changes in News Language in British Newspapers, 1880–1930," *Media, Culture & Society* 22 (2000), 557–73.

4 Michael Schudson, "Question Authority: A History of the News Interview in American Journalism, 1860s–1930s," *Media, Culture & Society* 16 (1994), 565–87. Reprinted in Michael Schudson, *The Power of News* (Cambridge, MA: Harvard University Press, 1995), pp. 72–93.

5 Tim P. Vos, "Journalists' Endangered Professional Status," *Journalism: Theory, Practice and Criticism* 20, no. 1 (2019), 122–5.

6 Joseph Pulitzer, "The College of Journalism," *North American Review* 178, no. 570 (1904), 641–80 at 680.

7 Ibid., 657.

8 Ibid., 649.

9 Cited in Margaret Sullivan, "Media Must 'Fight Their Own DNA' to Properly Cover the Redacted Mueller Report," *Washington Post*, April 17, 2019.

10 Marcel Broersma, "Americanization, or: the Rhetoric of Modernity. How European Journalism Adapted US Norms, Practices and Convention," in Klaus Arnold, Paschal Preston, and Susanne Kinnebrock, eds., *Handbook of European Communication History* (Chichester and Malden, MA: Wiley, 2020), p. 411.

11 Ibid.

12 Ibid., p. 416.

13 Karin Wahl-Jorgensen, "The Strategic Ritual of Emotionality: A Case Study of Pulitzer Prize-winning

Articles," *Journalism: Theory, Practice and Criticism* 14, no. 1 (2013), 129–45.

14 Al Tompkins, *Aim for the Heart: Write, Shoot, Report and Produce for TV and Multimedia*, 2nd edition (Washington, DC: CQ Press, 2012).

15 Cited in Rachel Smolkin, "The Women," *American Journalism Review* (December 2003–January 2004) at https://ajrarchive.org/article.asp?id=3507.

16 December 15, 2016, BBC *Newsnight* interview with Ian Katz. Cited in Rusbridger, *Breaking News*, p. 253.

17 Jack Goldsmith, "Interview with Dean Baquet, Executive Editor of *New York Times*, on Publication Decisions About Intelligence Secrets, and More," April 29, 2015, *Lawfare* Blog at https://www.law fareblog.com/jack-goldsmiths-interview-dean-ba quet-executive-editor-new-york-times-publication-de cisions-about.

18 Bob Woodward, *Veil: The Secret Wars of the CIA, 1981–1987* (New York: Pocket Books, 1988), pp. 516–35.

19 David E. McCraw, *Truth in Our Times* (New York: All Points Books, 2019), p. 195.

20 Jack Newfield, "Journalism: Old, New and Corporate," in Ronald Weber, ed., *The Reporter as Artist: A Look at the New Journalism* (New York: Hastings House, 1974), p. 56. This reprints an essay originally published in 1970.

21 Herbert Gans, *Deciding What's News* (New York: Pantheon Books, 1979).

22 I cite here from C. W. Anderson, Leonard Downie

Jr., and Michael Schudson, *The News Media: What Everyone Needs to Know* (New York: Oxford University Press, 2016), p. 112. In this section of this co-authored book, Downie was the lead author. While the term "accountability journalism" has not replaced "muckraking" or "investigative reporting" or "watchdog journalism," all terms still in wider use, Downie began speaking of "accountability journalism" when he was still executive editor (1991–2008) of the *Washington Post*, and his emphasis that it is not limited to investigative reporting seems to me vital. He thinks he may have been the first or among the first to use the term – "I believe I was the first to use the term accountability journalism widely and often" – email, November 22, 2017). I find it the best term for the kind of journalism democracies need most.

23 Andrew Chadwick, Cristian Vaccari, and Ben O'Loughlin, "Do Tabloids Poison the Well of Social Media? Explaining Democratically Dysfunctional News Sharing," *New Media and Society* 20, no. 1 (2018), 4255–74 at 4270.

Chapter 3 Reported, Compelling, Assertive: Anatomy of Journalism That Matters

1 Erik Neveu, "News Without Journalists: Real Threat or Horror Story?" *Brazilian Journalism Research* 6, no. 1 (2010), 29–54 at 51.

2 Paul Starr, "The Edge of Social Science," *Harvard Educational Review* 44, no. 4 (1974), 393–415.

3 Stuart Hall, "The Determination of News Photographs" in Stanley Cohen and Jock Young, eds., *The Manufacture of News: A Reader* (Beverly Hills: Sage, 1973), pp. 176–90; and Gaye Tuchman, "Objectivity as Strategic Ritual: An Examination of Newsmen's Notions of Objectivity," *American Journal of Sociology* 77 (1972), 660–79.

4 Johan Galtung and Mari Ruge, "The Structure of Foreign News: The Presentation of the Congo, Cuba and Cyprus Crises in Four Foreign Newspapers," in Jeremy Tunstall, ed., *Media Sociology: A Reader* (Urbana: University of Illinois Press, 1970), pp. 259–98.

5 Wahl-Jorgensen, "The Strategic Ritual of Emotionality" and also *Emotions, Media and Politics* (Cambridge: Polity, 2019).

6 Jack Fuller, *What Is Happening to News: The Information Explosion and the Crisis in Journalism* (Chicago: University of Chicago Press, 2010), p. 169.

7 Katherine Brown, *Your Country, Our War: The Press and Diplomacy in Afghanistan* (New York: Oxford University Press, 2019), pp. 87–9.

8 The key study on this is Silvio Waisbord, *Watchdog Journalism in South America* (New York: Columbia University Press, 2000). The quoted passage is from p. xiii.

9 Silvio Waisbord, personal communication, June 7, 2019.

10 Steven E. Clayman, Marc M. Elliott, John Heritage, and Megan K. Beckett, "A Watershed in White House Journalism: Explaining the Post-1968

Rise of Aggressive Presidential News," *Political Communication* 27 (2010), 229–47.

11 Katherine Fink and Michael Schudson, "The Rise of Contextual Reporting, 1950s–2000s," *Journalism: Theory, Practice and Criticism* 15, no. 1 (2014), 3–20.

Chapter 4 The Problem of Media Bias

1 Samuel G. Freedman with Kerry Donahue, *Dying Words: The AIDS Reporting of Jeff Schmalz and How It Transformed the New York Times* (New York: CUNY Journalism Press, 2015), p. 10.

2 Albert C. Gunther, "Biased Press or Biased Public? Attitudes Toward Media Coverage of Social Groups," *Public Opinion Quarterly* 56, no. 2 (1992), 147–67 at 163.

3 John Carreyrou, *Bad Blood: Secrets and Lies in a Silicon Valley Startup* (New York: Alfred A. Knopf, 2019), pp. 269–70.

4 Meg Greenfield, *Washington* (New York: Public Affairs, 2001), p. 124; and Lynn Povich, *The Good Girls Revolt: How the Women of Newsweek Sued Their Bosses and Changed the Workplace* (New York: Public Affairs, 2012), p. 216.

5 Povich, *The Good Girls Revolt*, p. 201.

6 Eleanor Holmes Norton, quoted in ibid., p. 216.

Chapter 5 Evidence That Journalism Matters
(or Doesn't)

1 Kenneth Newton, *Surprising News: How the Media Affect – and Do Not Affect – Politics* (Boulder, CO: Lynne Rienner, 2019), p. 7.

2 Markus Prior, *Post-Broadcast Democracy: How Media Choice Increases Inequality in Political Involvement and Polarizes Elections* (Cambridge: Cambridge University Press, 2007). See also Newton, *Surprising News*, pp. 204–8.

3 Hannah Arendt, "Truth and Politics," in *Between Past and Future* (New York: Viking Press, 1968), p. 161.

4 James Boylan "Declarations of Independence," *Columbia Journalism Review* 25, no. 4 (1986), 29–45.

5 Fareed Zakaria, "The Rise of Illiberal Democracy," *Foreign Affairs* 76, no. 6 (1997), 22–43.

6 Paul Dickson, *Authorisms: Words Wrought by Writers* (New York: Bloomsbury, 2014), p. 48 for "Cold War' and p. 111 for "middle America."

7 Newton, *Surprising News*, p. 192.

8 Martin L. Brown and Arnold L. Potosky, "The Presidential Effect: The Public Health Response to Media Coverage About Ronald Reagan's Colon Cancer Episode," *Public Opinion Quarterly* 54, no. 3 (1990), 317–29.

9 Peter van Aelst, Kjersti Thorbjornsrud, and Toril Aalberg, "The Political Information Environment During Election Campaigns," in Toril Aalberg and

James Curran, eds., *How Media Inform Democracy* (New York: Routledge, 2012), pp. 50–63.

10 Michael Schudson, *Why Democracies Need an Unlovable Press* (Cambridge: Polity, 2008), pp. 17–20.

11 Bernard Manin, *The Principles of Representative Government* (Cambridge: Cambridge University Press, 1997), pp. 218–35.

Chapter 6 Why Technology is Not the Whole Story

1 This account follows Ian Hutchby, "Technology, Texts and Affordances," *Sociology* 35, no. 2 (2001), 441–56.

2 Ann Blair, "Reading Strategies for Coping with Information Overload ca. 1550–1700," *Journal of the History of Ideas* 64, no. 1 (2003), 11–28.

3 Wolfgang Behringer, "Communications Revolutions: A Historiographical Concept," *German History* 24, no. 3 (2006), 333–74 at 342.

4 See a good discussion of this in Rachel Smolkin, "Cities Without Newspapers," *American Journalism Review* 31, no. 3 (2009), 16–25.

5 Rasmus Kleis Nielsen, "The Many Crises of Western Journalism: A Comparative Analysis of Economic Crises, Professional Crises, and Crises of Confidence," in Jeffrey C. Alexander, Elizabeth Butler Breese, and Maria Luengo, eds., *The Crisis of Journalism Reconsidered: Democratic Culture, Professional Codes, Digital Future* (Cambridge: Cambridge University Press, 2016), pp. 77–97 at p. 95.

6 David Carr, "Papers are Down, and Now Out," *New York Times*, August 11, 2014.

7 I attended the conference and these are Carr's words as I remember them. The conference was at Yale Law School, November 13–14, 2009, "The Future of Journalism: Who Will Pay the Messengers?"

8 Newton, *Surprising News*, p. 172.

9 Carl Sessions Stepp, "The State of the American Newspaper: Then and Now," *American Journalism Review* 21 (1999), 60–75 at 62. See also other relevant references in Katherine Fink and Michael Schudson, "The Rise of Contextual Journalism, 1950s–2000s," *Journalism: Theory, Criticism, Practice* 15, no. 1 (2014), 3–20.

10 Marcel Broersma, "The Legitimacy Paradox." *Journalism: Theory, Criticism and Practice* 20, no. 1 (2019), 92–4 at 92.

11 Beth Knobel, *The Watchdog Still Barks: How Accountability Reporting Evolved for the Digital Age* (New York: Fordham University Press, 2018), p. 13.

Chapter 7 Journalism's Four Non-Revolutions

1 Fuller, *What Is Happening to News*, pp. 6–7, 12.

2 Rusbridger, *Breaking News*, pp. xx–xxiii.

3 Monika Djerf-Pierre and Adam Shebata, "Still an Agenda Setter: Traditional News Media and Public Opinion During the Transition from Low to High Choice Media Environments," *Journal of Communication* 6 (2017), 733–57.

4 See Nikki Usher, *Making News at the New York Times* (Ann Arbor: University of Michigan Press, 2014).

5 Pew Research Center, "Amid Criticism, Support for Media's 'Watchdog' Role Stands Out" (August 8, 2013), p. 13, https://www.people-press.org/2013/08/08/amid-criticism-support-for-medias-watchdog-role-stands-out/. Based on a survey conducted July 17–21, 2013.

6 Peter Berglez and Amanda Gearing, "The Panama and Paradise Papers: The Rise of a Global Fourth Estate," *International Journal of Communication* 12 (2018), 44573–92.

7 Katherine Fink and C. W. Anderson, "Data Journalism in the United States: Beyond the Usual Suspects," *Journalism Studies* 16, no. 4 (2015), 467–81.

8 Nicholas John, "Sharing," in Benjamin Peters, ed., *Digital Keywords* (Princeton: Princeton University Press, 2016), pp. 269–77. See also Nicholas John, *The Age of Sharing* (Cambridge: Polity, 2017).

9 Damian Trilling, Petro Tolochko, and Björn Burscher, "From Newsworthiness to Shareworthiness: How to Predict News Sharing Based on Article Characteristics," *Journalism & Mass Communication Quarterly* 94, no. 1 (2017), 38–60.

10 Aaron Smith, "Many Facebook Users Don't Understand How the Site's News Feed Works," Pew Research Center, September 5, 2018, https://www.pewresearch.org/fact-tank/2018/09/05/many-facebook-users-dont-understand-how-the-sites-news-feed-works/.

11 Silvio Waisbord and Adriana Amado, "Populist Communication by Digital Means: Presidential Twitter in Latin America," *Information, Communication & Society* 20, no. 9 (2017), 1330–46.

12 John Durham Peters, *Speaking into the Air: A History of the Idea of Communication* (Chicago: University of Chicago Press, 1999), p. 34.

Chapter 8 Is There a Future for Journalism?

1 Elana Beiser, "Hundreds of Journalists Jailed Globally Becomes the New Normal," Committee to Protect Journalists, December 13, 2018, https://cpj.org/reports/2018/12/journalists-jailed-imprisoned-turkey-china-egypt-saudi-arabia.php.

2 Interview, June 26, 2019.

3 Lucas Graves, "Boundaries Not Drawn: Mapping the Institutional Roots of the Global Fact-Checking Movement," *Journalism Studies* 19, no. 5 (2018), 613–31; Mark Stencel, "Number of Fact-Checking Outlets Surges to 188 in More Than 60 Countries," Duke Reporters' Lab, June 11, 2019, https://www.poynter.org/fact-checking/2019/number-of-fact-checking-outlets-surges-to-188-in-more-than-60-countries/; and Lucas Graves, personal communication, September 13, 2019.

4 Carreyrou, *Bad Blood*, p. 223.

5 Brown, *Your Country, Our War*, p. 78.

6 Rusbridger, *Breaking News*, p. 158.

7 Lynn Schofield Clark and Regina Marchi, *Young*

People and the Future of News: Social Media and the Rise of Connective Journalism (Cambridge: Cambridge University Press, 2017), p. 163.

8 Jürgen Habermas, *The Structural Transformation of the Public Sphere: An Inquiry into a Category of Bourgeois Society*, trans. Thomas Burger (Cambridge, MA: MIT Press, 1991).

9 Robert Darnton, "An Early Information Society: News and the Media in Eighteenth-Century Paris," *American Historical Review* 105, no. 1 (2000), 1–35.

10 Julia Sonnevend, *Stories Without Borders: The Berlin Wall and the Making of a Global Iconic Event* (New York: Oxford University Press, 2016).

11 Walter Lippmann, *Public Opinion* (New York: Macmillan, 1922, 1965), p. 16.

Further Reading

With the rapid growth in the past two decades of "journalism studies" as a subfield of communication studies, there are a growing number of reference books that take up a great many topics about or closely related to journalism. Two are of special note as official publications of the International Communication Association, a leading and genuinely international scholarly association. One of these is the *The Handbook of Journalism Studies*, 2nd edition (London: Routledge, 2019), edited by Karin Wahl-Jorgensen and Thomas Hanitzsch. The other is the *International Encyclopedia of Journalism Studies*, edited by Folker Hanusch and Tim P. Vos (Oxford: Wiley Online Library, 2019).

There are a number of well-organized, high-quality collections of essays about journalism that are well worth consulting. These include, on journalism history, Richard R. John and Jonathan Silberstein-Loeb, eds., *Making News: The Political Economy of Journalism in Britain and America from the Glorious Revolution to the Internet* (Oxford: Oxford University Press, 2015), which is unusual in historical work on journalism in covering Britain and its American colonies, both in detail, with some attention to journalism in other parts of the British empire, too; and Bruce E. Schulman and Julian E. Zelizer, eds., *Media Nation: The Political History of News in Modern America* (Philadelphia: University of Pennsylvania Press, 2017). James Curran and David Hesmondhalgh, eds., *Media and Society*, 6th edition (London: Bloomsbury Academic, 2019) is impressively global in its reach. It covers contemporary "media" in general, not journalism alone, but several papers are devoted to journalism specifically. One more collection of note focuses specifically on the crisis or sense of crisis in contemporary journalism with both US and European examples: Jeffrey C. Alexander, Elizabeth Butler Breese, and Maria Luengo, eds., *The Crisis of Journalism Reconsidered* (Cambridge: Cambridge University Press, 2016).

The single most useful concept to reckon with in my view of journalism is "profession" or "professionalism." On journalism as a profession, see Silvio

Further Reading

Waisbord, *Reinventing Professionalism: Journalism and News in Global Perspective* (Cambridge: Polity, 2013). But note also Barbie Zelizer's well-argued critique of using the concept of a profession to characterize journalism: "Journalists as Interpretive Communities," *Critical Studies in Mass Communication* 10 (1993), 219–37. She makes a case that journalism should be understood as an "interpretive community" as well as a profession. It remains a thoughtful, even eloquent, paper more than 25 years after publication.

All of these recommendations are written for academic audiences. Less forbidding would be works designed expressly for a general audience, including, notably, memoirs. Katharine Graham's memoir of her life, concentrating on her long tenure as publisher of the *Washington Post*, is a classic: *Personal History* (New York: Random House, 1997). Less well known but a delight to read concerning both Washington politics and politicians and journalism is Meg Greenfield, *Washington* (New York: Public Affairs, 2001). An excellent read, cited several times in this book, is Alan Rusbridger's memoir of his career in British journalism: *Breaking News: The Remaking of Journalism and Why It Matters Now* (New York: Farrar Straus Giroux, 2018).

The best work I know on what journalism should

be, how ethical journalists should report and write the news, how they should act in the newsroom and out, is Bill Kovach and Tom Rosenstiel, *The Elements of Journalism: What Newspeople Should Know and the Public Should Expect*, 3rd edition (New York: Three Rivers Press, 2014). It is very accessible to the general reader. Although 2014 seems a long time ago on a digital clock and no doubt the book could use another update, it's still relevant to journalists today and a window on how two leading American journalists think about their vocation.